I
LOVE
TIMES
I Love Type Series
Volume Eight

Published
by Viction:ary

Edited & Designed
by TwoPoints.Net

THE MONOTYPE RECORDER

SPECIAL ISSUE DESCRIBING

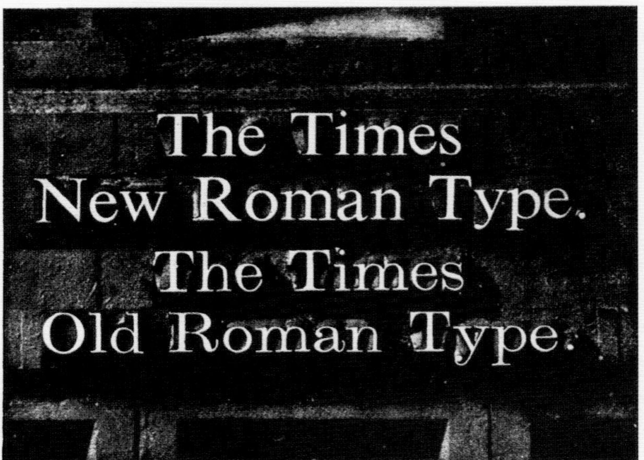

LONDON
THE MONOTYPE CORPORATION LIMITED
43 FETTER LANE, E.C. 4

The controversy surrounding the origins of the Times New Roman® typeface and a typeface supposedly commissioned by the 19th century industrial designer, Starling Burgess, has been rebounding around the type community for more than a dozen years. The suggestion is that Monotype did not have the rights to use the design and that; therefore, Times New Roman should not be considered part of the Monotype Library. There has never been definitive evidence to prove that the Burgess design was the basis for Times New Roman. The Burgess story suggests he commissioned Lanston Monotype, in the United States, to develop a custom font based on design input from him. The design commission was not finalized and, if this were the case, Lanston Monotype would have owned all the work that was done on the face. Supposedly, Lanston Monotype sent the patters and punchsetter cards to Monotype in the UK. (Although there is no record of this particular transfer – sharing intellectual property was common between the two branches of the Monotype Company). If the intellectual property was sent to Monotype in the U.K., and Stanley Morison based one of his design proposals for the Times newspaper on the Lanston face, the resulting design would still have been the property of Monotype. Several design proposals to the Times newspaper in the early 1930s were based on existing designs. This was not an uncommon process in the development of a custom font then – or now.

Steeped in tradition, the Times New Roman® family has been described as one of the most familiar and successful typefaces in the world – it has also been used for just about every typographic application imaginable. The typeface was born, however, out of controversy.

In 1929, when the advertising manager of The Times newspaper in London asked the young Stanley Morison's opinion about approaching Monotype to take out an ad in a special edition of the paper, Morison's reply was blunt and startling. He said that he would rather pay The Times a large sum of money to keep their hands off a Monotype advertisement. Morison, who was a consultant to Monotype at the time, went on to give the manager a short lecture on the bad printing and out-of-date typography of his newspaper. These criticisms were reported to the Managing Director of The Times who, in turn, reached out to Morison and asked him to explain what he thought should be done to improve the publication. Morison replied that nothing short of a complete redesign of the entire typography of the paper would suffice. Impressed by the force and insight with which Morison argued his case, the Managing Director proceeded to hire Morison as typographical adviser to the newspaper.

As part of his first actions with the new responsibility, Morison decided that a completely new typeface was also needed for The Times. A special committee was appointed by the newspaper to "consider the desirability of making an alteration in the typefaces currently being used". Morison, however, was the driving force of the complete project from its inception to its final conclusion. This is confirmed by the fact that he went ahead with his ideas for a new type without confiding with any of the committee members. On his own, he prepared a detailed report outline what kind of typeface was needed – complete with trial setting in a new custom designed typeface to show the committee.

The criteria Morison set for the new design was deceptively simple: the typeface would have to appear larger than its predecessor, could take up no more space, should be slightly heavier and, ultimately, must be highly legible. After some consideration, he decided that the new design should be based on the Plantin, a typeface cut in the 16th century by Robert Granjon and used by Plantin-Moretus Press in the 17th century. Morison called his new typeface, "Times New Roman" to differentiate it from the previously used design.

The steps that led to the first drawing of this type are, however, obscure and a number of theories have been produced as to its origins; including one suggestion that it was based on a design commissioned by the American industrial designer, Starling Burgess.

Morison added to the confusion by writing in 1953 that he drew a set of drawings and handed them to Victor Lardent, of The Times publicity department, and that Lardent made finished drawings based on pencil sketches he provided. Lardent, however, recalled that it was a much lengthier process – and that no pencil sketches were involved. He said that Morison initially handed him a photographic copy of a page from a book set in the original Plantin type to use as a basis. Lardent then drew the base characters, and Morison edited and art directed the design until he was satisfied with the end results.

Since The Times used both Monotype and Linotype machines to set type for its issues, a second, almost identical design, was produced by Linotype for their typesetters. The Times Roman® typeface was the result of this design effort. Over the years, Times New Roman and its nearly twin sister have been translated into virtually every kind of font.

The Times New Roman design enjoyed another surge of popularity when it became one of the staple of typefaces routinely bundled with computer operating systems and productivity software.

There are few situations outside of Times New Roman's range of usage. It is an exceptional typeface that has been used to set books, periodicals, annual reports, brochures – and, yes, even newspapers. In addition, Times New Roman has also been used to set display typography from an inch high to several feet.

Allan Haley
Director of Words & Letters
Monotype

To all probability no typeface has ever been in the same position as Times (or Times New Roman) is today. There have been other popular typefaces that became something of a default choice to their users, printing and typesetting shops; but that was before computers replaced the pen and the typewriter, before composing and printing text became something everybody can do. Since the advent of personal computers, Times has been used to design everything and anything: books, art journals and catalogs, scientific papers, memos, letters, lost-dog leaflets, tart cards, shop lettering. It was also the default serif font for websites for over a decade. Consequently, for designers and non-professional users alike, Times has become a kind of "non-choice". Times' sans-serif companion as a standard system font is Helvetica, but Helvetica's story is a bit different. For one thing, on many computers it was never the default sans-serif because of its competitor Arial, which was designed for Microsoft as a cheap Helvetica alternative. More importantly, the real Helvetica has always remained a classy choice among highbrow designers, especially for corporate identities; and it regained an undeniable hipness after Neville Brody chose it for his design of the magazine *Arena* it the late 1980s. Times, on the other hand, went through a period in which it was neither fashionable nor an obvious option for mainstream designers (except for those making safe choices for a newspaper redesign). Its very ubiquity made it a face that was tolerated rather than loved.

Then, slowly but surely, the blandness of Times became part of a design strategy — or should I say: a non-design strategy? I noticed this first when working in the cultural field in early 1990s Belgium. Contrary to their Dutch neighbors, Flemish cultural institutions had very small budgets for publications, and not much of a design tradition; consequently, catalogs were often laid out by artists, gallerists and even museum curators. The consensus seemed to be that these books and brochures had to look as "undesigned" as possible; any fancy typography would have been seen as an attempt to steal the show from the works of art. Times New Roman became the typeface of choice. When a Flemish art foundation began publishing a highly intellectual and subsequently very influential magazine called *De Witte Raaf* (White Raven), it followed suit with an austere design using exclusively Times.

In the course of the 1990s, ever more people became interested in digital type. Type design first became an area of experimentation, almost an art form in itself, with designers adapting postmodernist principles to their craft: citation, appropriation, sampling, parody. Soon, these same designers and their younger peers embraced tradition and honed their skills, coming up with serious fonts that were increasingly refined. In a rebellious reaction to all that typographic sophistication, cutting-edge graphic designers began to turn away from contemporary type design. They abandoned the quest for the ultimate new, well-wrought typeface for a much more elementary desire: they wanted type without a face. Their approach wasn't new; designers in the 1920s had argued in favor of "impersonal" and even "uninteresting" typefaces; post-1945 functionalism had used terms like "neutrality" and "objectivity". But invariably, these ideological motives had always led to a choice of technical sans-serifs: Akzidenz, Univers, Helvetica, or the somewhat more romantic geometry of Futura and Kabel. When, around 2000, the design avant-garde embraced Times, the unassuming system font, as a typeface for contrary graphic statements, this was quite a new way of defining objectivity and neutrality in type selection.

Slowly but surely, Times became a major typographic tool in what is now often referred to as "hipster design". This was and still is a graphic approach that makes deliberate use of certain characteristics of non-professional, vernacular digital layout that academic modernism likes to renounce as bad practice — centered text, double, triple or quadruple emphasis (e.g. bold italic capitals, underlined), black ink on pink or baby-blue stock, etc. The use of Times completed the picture perfectly: a typeface that serious typographers had all but abandoned, but which amateurs liked to use because it looks familiar and serious — and is free. The effect has been rather astonishing. In the course of about ten years, in the young designer's subconsciousness, using Times went from being an ironic non-choice (or even a decision to embrace ugliness) to an option that connotes hipness and contemporary sensibility. What was initially anti-design — a mischievous, dada-like refusal to make any typographic statement at all — gradually became almost the opposite: a shortcut to stylishness.

Like other media in art and design, typefaces go through appreciation cycles. In postmodern times (i.e., since the early 1980s) these cycles have become increasingly complex and subtle. One factor that confuses the issue is that there are so many graphic subcultures that have conflicting habits and codes. The exact same design decision — a color, a certain arrangement, the choice of a typeface — may have opposite meanings in different contexts. There is a kind "contemporaneity of the non-contemporary" that causes certain stylistic means to look old-fashioned or soulless to one person or group, and totally cool to another. As for Times, perhaps the joke has worn thin, as it had some years ago with OCR typefaces in an artsy context. On the computer, Times is being replaced by standard fonts of a different calibre: On the web, Georgia is far superior to Times, and is still gaining in popularity; Lucas de Groot's sans-serif Calibri has been designed to roughly follow Times' metrics, so that it can painlessly replace the rather skinny oldstyle face that was so unfortunately chosen, 20 years ago, to be an internet star.

So, Times New Roman will soon shed its aura of blandness and banality, and be able to reclaim its rightful place among classic oldstyle fonts. It's not the most elegant or harmonious family but it has an unmistakable charisma that is most obvious when seen in its earlier incarnations as a metal typeface. Perhaps there will be revised digital editions that bring back that sparkle. Discerning typographic designers will be able to have a fresh look at the hybrid structure and ambiguous detailing of Times New Roman, and say: Yeah, it's actually a pretty interesting typeface.

Jan Middendorp
Author of Dutch Type, Shaping Text, Hand to Type, etc., Editor for MyFonts. Co-editor of Type Navigator.

FANTASTIC MAN

PROFILE

Mr.
FRANCESCO
VEZZOLI

THE ARTIST
of high concept films, fabulous friends and plenty of airmiles...

Text .... Tim Blanks
Photography and styling .... Matthias Vriens

FANTASTIC MAN

PROFILE

Mr.
VAN SANT

Mr. GUS VAN SANT
Meeting the incredible director as he finishes his long-awaited new movie MILK...

Text .... Ryan Gilbey
Photography .... Bryan Adams
Styling .... Maryam Malakpour

a

Fantastic Man
2005-12 — Editorial Design, Visual Identity
Client Top Publishers
Design Jop van Bennekom, Veronica Ditting

FANTASTIC MAN is the original gentleman's journal, obsessed with personal style, intelligent writing and eloquent photography. The magazine contains interviews and fashion features with inspiring men and interesting personalities. It features men in clothes rather than models in fashion. FANTASTIC MAN's take on fashion is a very personal one, starting with personalities and the way they dress, it maps personal clothing and style. Contributing photographers are Alasdair McLellan, Willy Vanderperre, Juergen Teller, Mauric Scheltens & Liesbeth Abbenes and many others.

Jop van Bennekom & Veronica Ditting's Favorite Times Letter is "a".

"It's a classic; readable and versatile."

FANTASTIC
MAN
THE GENTLEMAN'S STYLE JOURNAL ... ISSUE N° 8 ... AUTUMN AND WINTER 2008
Mr. FRANCESCO VEZZOLI
The dream career of an international art star...
And ... Mr. GUS VAN SANT ... Mr. FERGUS HENDERSON ... Mr. TYLER BRÛLÉ ...
Mr. BONNIE "PRINCE" BILLY
FR / BE / NL - € 8.95
UK - £ 6.50
DE - € 10
AT / GR / ES / IT / Port.Cont. - € 9.90
9 771574 897006 08

FANTASTIC
MAN
Mr. EWAN McGREGOR
Back to work...
This 10th issue of THE GENTLEMAN'S STYLE JOURNAL for autumn and winter 2009 also features the noted make-up artist Mr. PETER PHILIPS, the scientist Dr. HANS ROSLING, the delightful Mr. HAMISH BOWLES, and many more. Plus... Introducing THE GENTLEWOMAN, the zero issue of FANTASTIC MAN's new girlfriend. Nice!

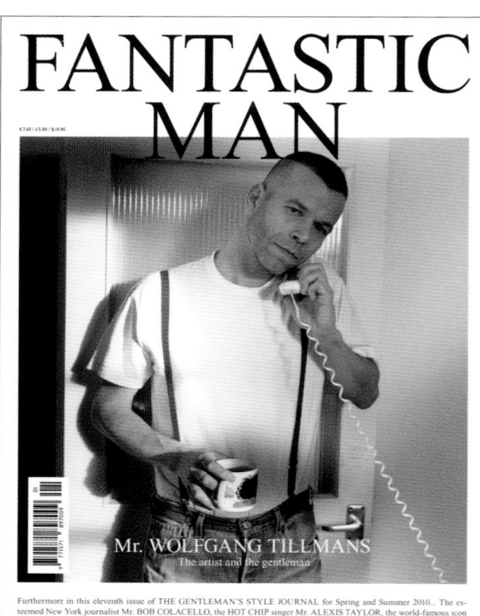
FANTASTIC
MAN
Mr. WOLFGANG TILLMANS
The artist and the gentleman
Furthermore in this eleventh issue of THE GENTLEMAN'S STYLE JOURNAL for Spring and Summer 2010... The esteemed New York journalist Mr. BOB COLACELLO, the HOT CHIP singer Mr. ALEXIS TAYLOR, the world-famous icon of masculinity FABIO, plus so much more to enjoy while travelling or at home in the garden.

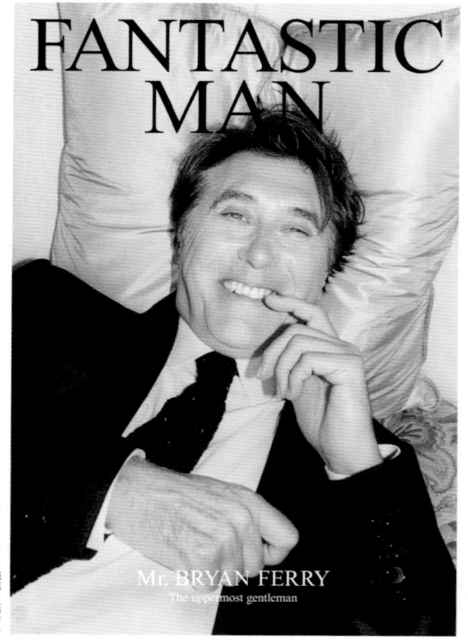
FANTASTIC
MAN
Mr. BRYAN FERRY
The uppermost gentleman

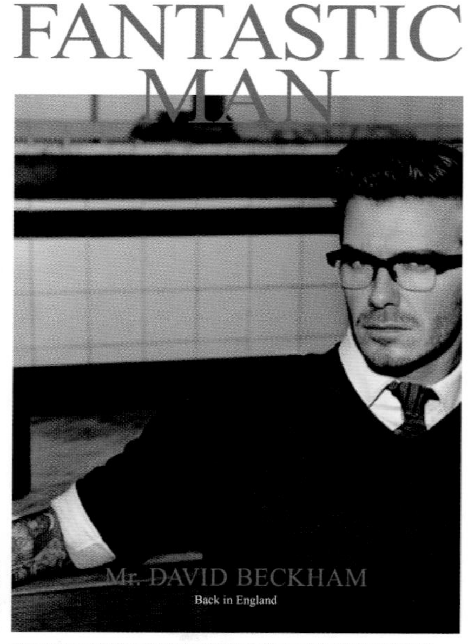
FANTASTIC
MAN
Mr. DAVID BECKHAM
Back in England
Furthermore in this 13th issue of FANTASTIC MAN: the media oligarch Mr. EVGENY LEBEDEV, the new director of TATE MODERN, Mr. CHRIS DERCON, and the famous Mr. MICHAEL STIPE

THE GENTLEMAN'S STYLE JOURNAL

ISSUE N° 14, AUTUMN & WINTER 2011

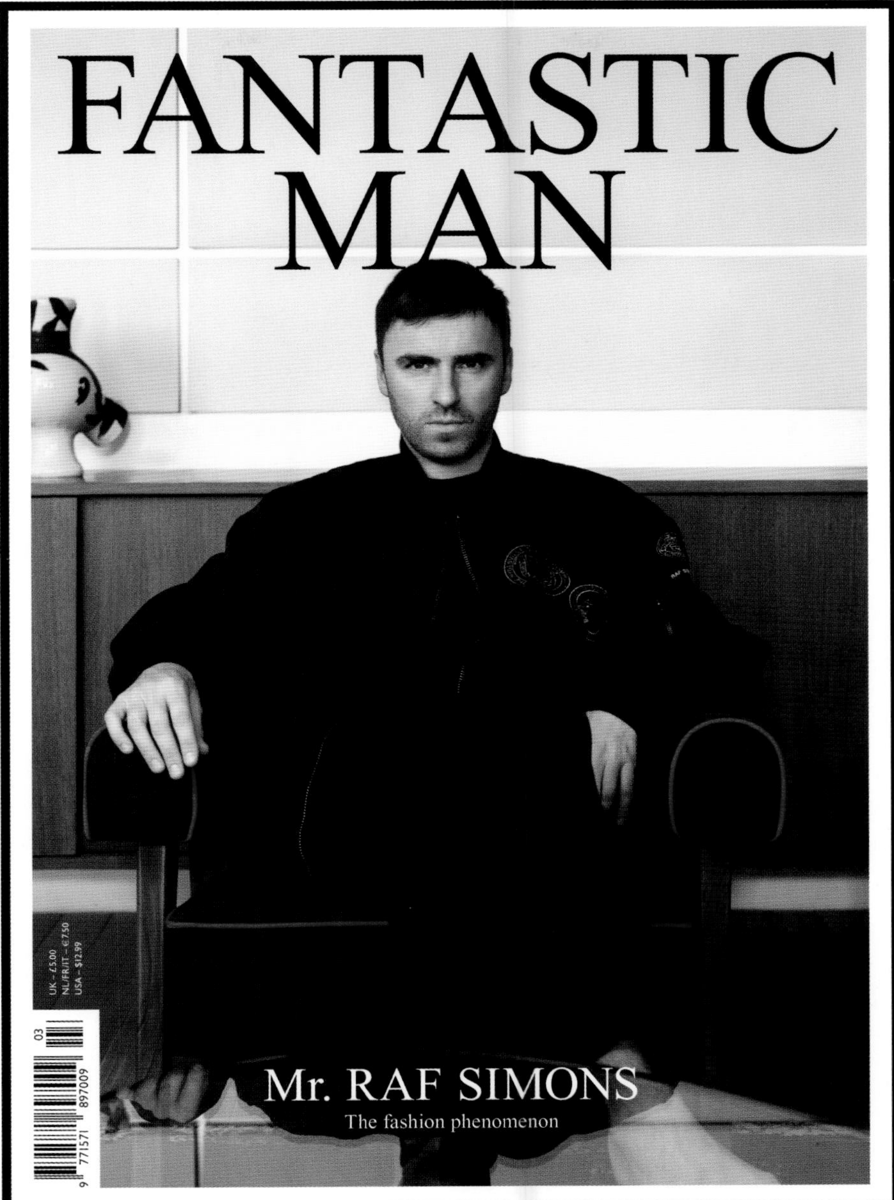

FANTASTIC MAN

("She was annoyed, because I had nothing to do.")

When he says he had nothing to do, it's as if Mr. AI is excusing himself for doing whatever he's done, and has done it despite himself. He says it with humility, and perhaps there are fatalistic tendencies at work: "Life is unpredictable and has unexpected effects," he emails me at one point. It helps explain his vulnerability to distractions—say, an activist who's been stranded by the police in the mountains and needs to be saved. But maybe it's also his way of defusing the criticism that he can seem like a celebrity artist, that he's a bit overeager to give his audiences what they expect and want.

Therein may lie the biggest irony. If one takes him at his word, Mr. AI has never wanted to be known as a Chinese artist per se. "In the '80s, when ALLEN GINSBERG read me his poetry, and I showed him my portfolio, he said, 'WEI-WEI, I can't think of a gallery that wants to show Chinese artists' work,'" Mr. AI recalls. "At that time, it bothered me. I said, 'ALLEN, I don't think of you as an American poet. You're just a poet.'"

What's more, Mr. AI is a champion of what he considers to be universal values. "The only thing I would not accept is regional thinking, because with today's globalisation and the internet, the world is completely different," he emails me.

But at the same time, Mr. AI's resonance depends in large measure on the extent to which he mirrors one's feelings about China. While few question his integrity, his critics sometimes find him too quick to judge an evolving system that, given the long arc of history, has made dizzyingly rapid strides. On the other hand, his supporters see him as a voice for the underdog, a much-needed reality check for a nation at risk of complacency, of being blinded by its current success.

For some, there's also the otherness factor. That is to say, he feeds into fears about a rising power they don't fully understand. When Mr. AI brought those 1,001 Chinese people to DOCUMENTA, he tapped into the West's anxieties about being overrun by the Eastern giant. However, "My intention was focused on the 1,001 people and how this would affect their lives," he says. "Any work, especially one related to worlds as different as China and the West, can carry completely different, even contradictory, meanings. And in general, people can only approach the surface; this is very normal."

For him, he says, the piece was more about the process of making it, which included everything from an open call on the internet to securing passports for participants from Chinese minority groups who didn't have last names. Referencing Kassel's status as home of the BROTHERS GRIMM, he called the experiment FAIRYTALE.

That said, how Mr. AI's own story will turn out is impossible to predict. "I can't answer why the government still hasn't put me in jail, but I'm ready to face it," he says, laughing nervously. "I would encourage them to not put me in jail. But I have to be prepared."

Theories abound as to why Mr. AI has so far avoided imprisonment. One explanation goes that, while he criticises the government, he doesn't cross the line of questioning its legitimacy.

"That's wrong," he shoots back. "From the very beginning I questioned the legitimacy of the Communist Party, though I don't have to say it all the time."

Some people say he's protected by his family background.

"That's underestimating the system. Look what happened to my father, so what's that background for?"

Maybe it's that he's too established.

"Throughout Chinese history, even those in the highest positions could be punished."

At one point, I wonder if it's because he's avoided hyper-touchy subjects like Tibet. But then he tells me about the meeting, albeit back in 1989, that he had with the DALAI LAMA. ("He liked my beard.") So the most obvious answer, I think, would also help explain why he's talking to me: in effect, he's shielded by the international media.

"Could be. But I don't know, maybe that's also an illusion. No one's that influential."

He's probably right. Overestimating yourself is risky, since finding your limits often means it's already too late. But Mr. AI seems fearless, or at least brave enough to face fear. And then he says something that sounds truly hard to believe, at least coming from him: "You know, people forget you from one minute to the next."

(Ends)

Etcetera

Mr. AI WEIWEI first exhibited in 1979, as part of a group show in Beijing called THE STARS. Although the show barely happened, due to the authorities shutting it down prematurely, it was a momentous occasion: the first time that experimental artists had dared to exhibit in 30 years of communist rule. THE STARS group managed to exhibit a second time in 1980. Many see THE STARS as having laid the groundwork for what became the contemporary Chinese art scene. Thirty years later, AI has yet to be the subject of a retrospective at any major international art institution; his TATE MODERN commission is possibly his biggest project in the West yet. As with previous TURBINE HALL exhibitors like CARSTEN HÖLLER, OLAFUR ELIASSON and LOUISE BOURGEOIS, nothing about the installation will be revealed until the opening day, on 12 October 2010.

- 158 -

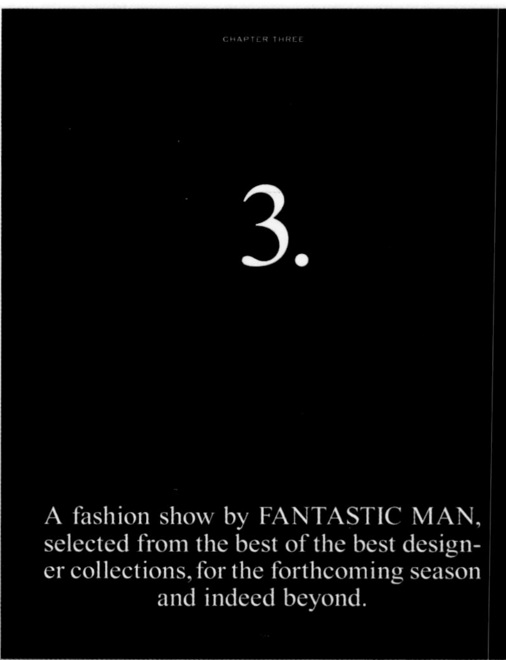

CHAPTER THREE
3.
A fashion show by FANTASTIC MAN, selected from the best of the best designer collections, for the forthcoming season and indeed beyond.

PROFILE

Mr. FEDERICO MARCHETTI

is the founder of YOOX, the super-successful shopping website that is now leading fashion to a whole new reality...

Text .... Caroline Roux
Photography .... Simon

- 95 -

Mr. DAVID WALLIAMS

is a British comedy actor whose fame has reached a whole new level, thanks to his recent marriage to fashion model Ms. LARA STONE, a new series with television partner Mr. MATT LUCAS, and a personal wardrobe that is the envy of them all...

Text .... Charlie Porter
Photography .... Alasdair McLellan

Presse Papier

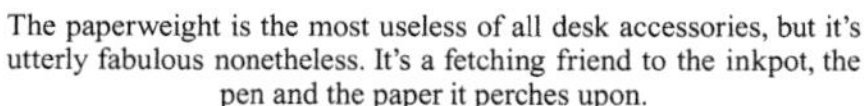

The paperweight is the most useless of all desk accessories, but it's utterly fabulous nonetheless. It's a fetching friend to the inkpot, the pen and the paper it perches upon.

Photography by Zoë Ghertner
Styling by Sam Logan

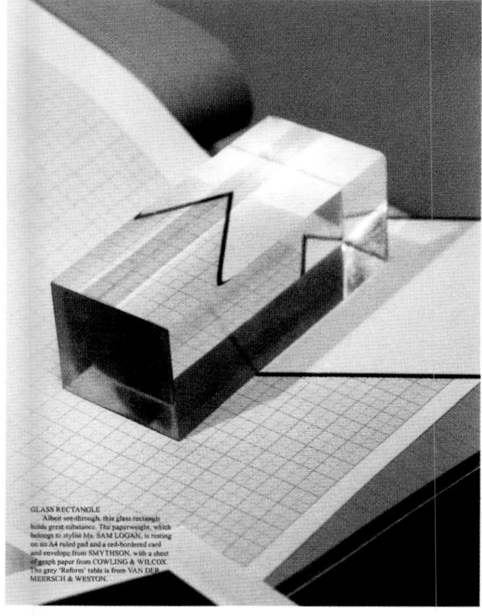

GLASS RECTANGLE
Albeit see-through, this glass rectangle holds great substance. The paperweight, which belongs to stylist Ms. SAM LOGAN, is resting on an A4 ruled pad and a red-bordered card and envelope from SMYTHSON, with a sheet of graph paper from COWLING & WILCOX. The grey 'Reform' table is from VAN DER MEERSCH & WESTON.

Index 1:20

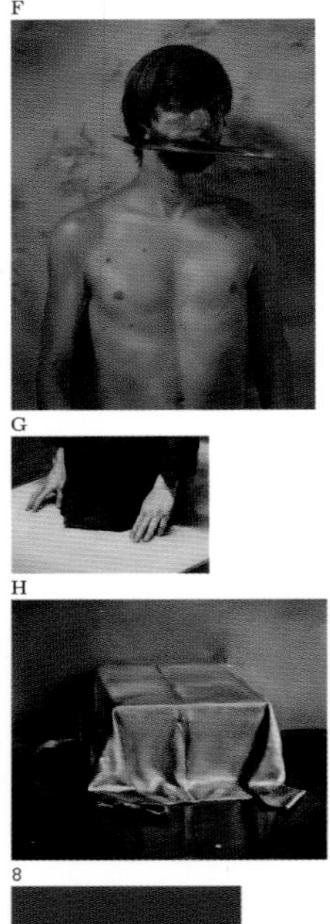

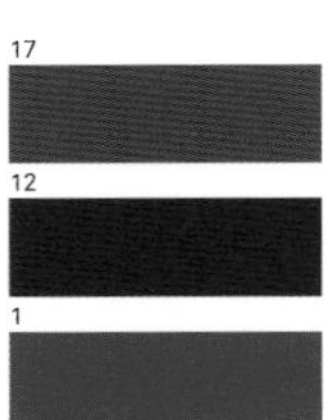

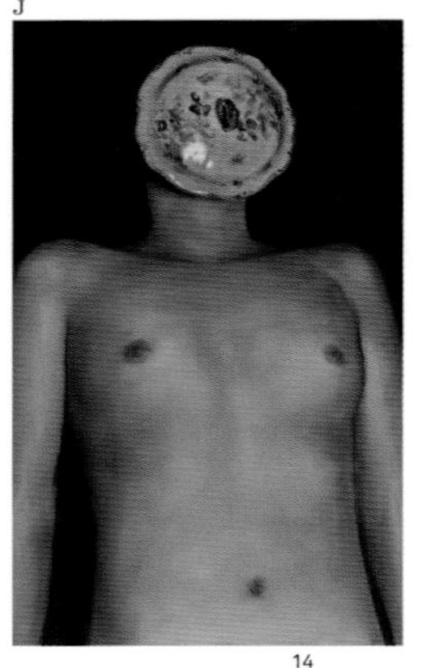

1

Anna Haas' Favorite Times Number is "1".

"I was looking for a neat, neutral and classic typeface. Times Eighteen is narrower and stiffer than Times New Roman. It suited the clean, but uncomfortable atmosphere of the paintings really well."

Michaël Borremans – Shades of Doubt
mono.kultur #31, Spring 2012
2012 — Publication
Client mono.kultur, Berlin
Design Anna Haas

mono.kulur is a quarterly interview magazine from Berlin. It deals with art and culture — or rather with the people who make them happen. In the foreground is music, film, literature. And image. And architecture. And media. mono.kultur features one interview per issue. Each time, another designer is giving the content its form. The only restrictions are the size of the magazine and the font, used for the "logo".

MONO.KULTUR #31 — Spring 2012

Michaël Borremans: Shades of Doubt

Index 1:20

A

18

4

11

B

16

C

D

E

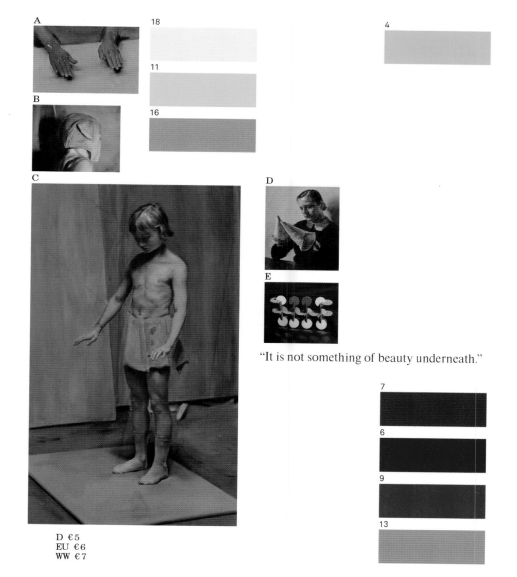

"It is not something of beauty underneath."

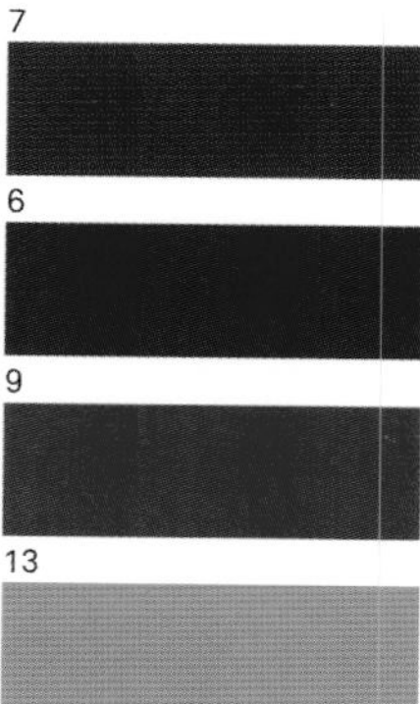

D €5
EU €6
WW €7

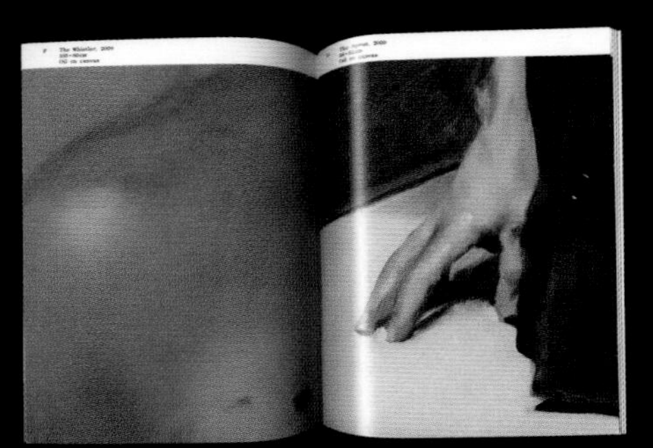

Michaël Borremans recently found a new way to kick off a productive day: One of his former assistants used to enjoy her morning coffee with a hint of vodka and some maple syrup, 'just a tiny, tiny bit of vodka, like 1:10, and then some syrup to sweeten it', and now the Belgian artist has also made it a habit to rely on the nameless drink's subtle power to 'open up your blood vessels'. Even so, his day's work still amounts to no more than what he calls 'low production'. Low it might seem – particularly to speculators who want to make easy money on the recent hype around Borremans' haunting paintings, drawings, and films. But low he shouldn't call it, as he knows all too well that he is very 'self-censoring' and will only let the best possible work, sometimes after multiple attempts and different versions, leave his combined home and workplace in Ghent. 'Low production' in his case simply means 'high standards'.

These high standards have, over the last decade, attracted more and more people to his work; nowadays, they even come to his house, unannounced, trying to snatch up a piece of the pie. But Michaël Borremans is an artist who is extremely devoted and loyal – to his galleries, to his ideas he calls 'ghosts', to his themes, to his entire vision and approach. He's a man who needs his pencil like he needs a smoke, who takes to drawing when others write in their diaries, and who treats his brushes and canvasses like a lover, going back and forth between moments of intense attraction

MONO.KULTUR #31 — Spring 2012
Michaël Borremans: Shades of Doubt
Index 1:20
"It is not something of beauty underneath."
D €5
EU €6
WW €7

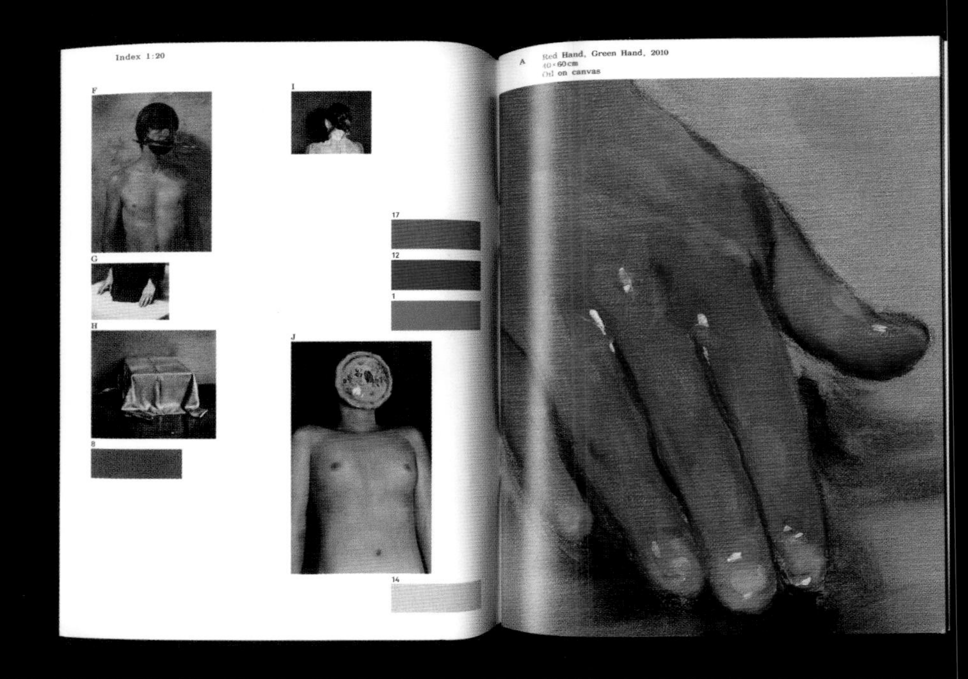
Index 1:20
Red Hand, Green Hand, 2010
40 × 60 cm
Oil on canvas

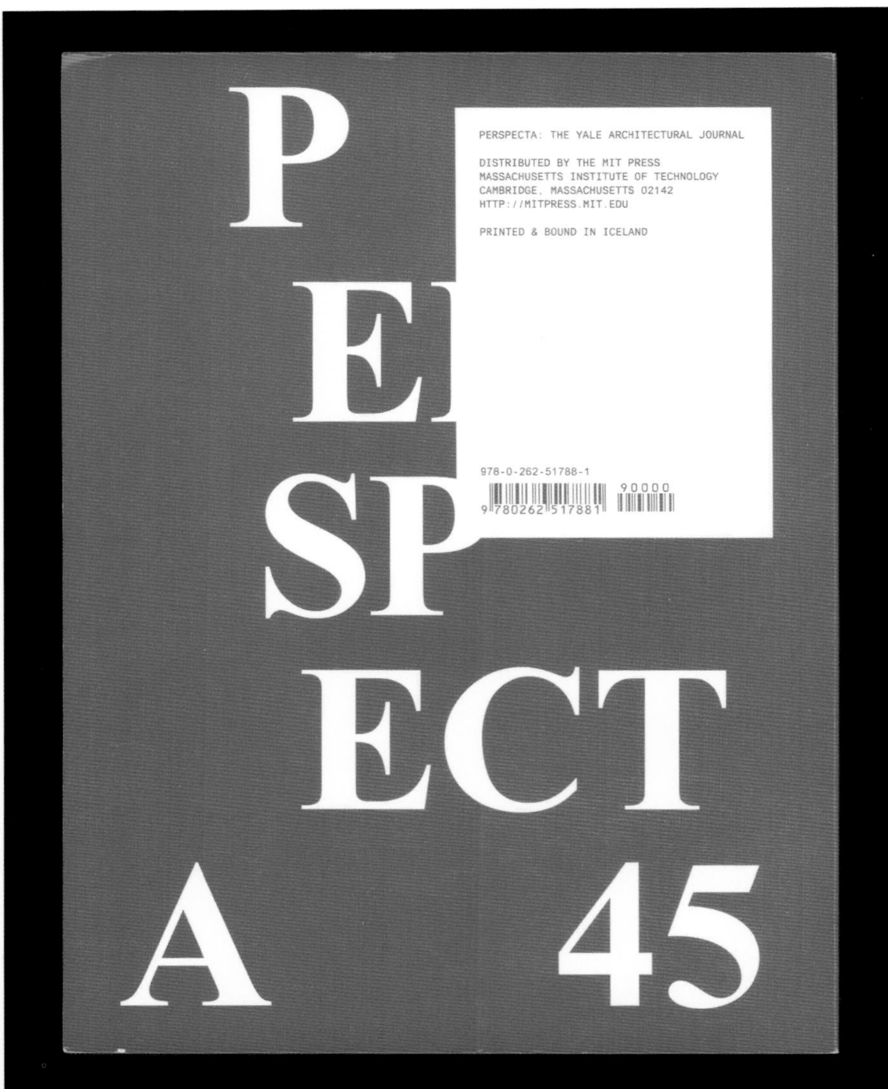

Perspecta 45: Agency
The Yale Architectural Journal
2012 — Publication, Identity
Client Yale School of Architecture
Design Mylinh Trieu Nguyen, Zak Jensen

Inspired by the issue's theme AGENCY, Times New Roman and Arial, both ubiquitous and often labeled "default" typefaces, were juxtaposed against each other to illustrate the dynamism between the often complex perception of the "old" and the "new." In these diverse configurations, the typefaces together produce a particular effect that encourages the reader to continually reevaluate the content.

Times New Roman Regular, Times New Roman Bold,
Times New Roman Condensed

A Conversation South of the Border

Metro Cable Car. Image courtesy of Urban-Think Tank and Daniel Schwartz

Urban-Think Tank

Alfredo Brillembourg and Hubert Klumpner
with research assistant Daniel Schwartz

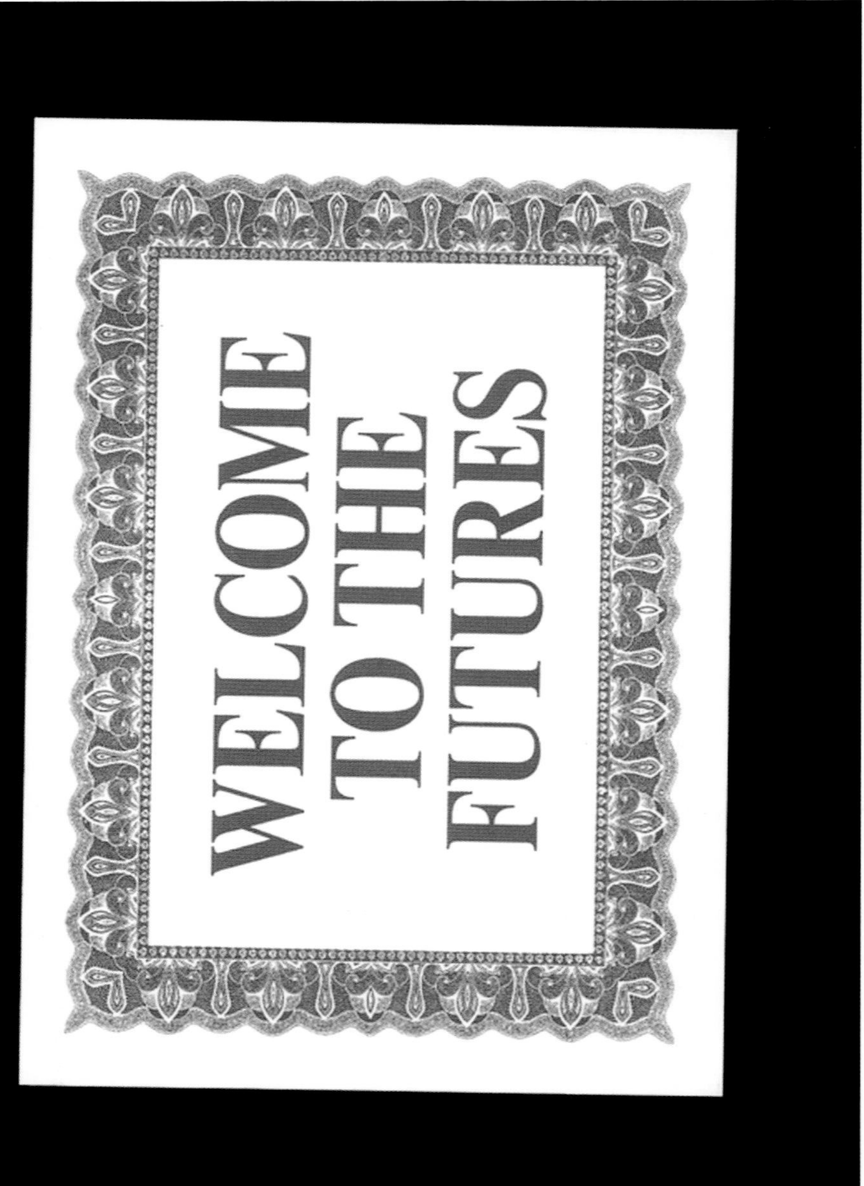

Investment Futures Strategy, Ltd.
The Book Trust Prospectus, Certificate of Authenticity
2010 — Certificate, Corporate Identity
Design Mylinh Trieu Nguyen, Benjamin Critton, Harry Gassel, Brendan Griffiths, Zak Klauck.

Typeface in Use
Times New Roman Regular,
Times New Roman Bold,
Times New Roman Condensed

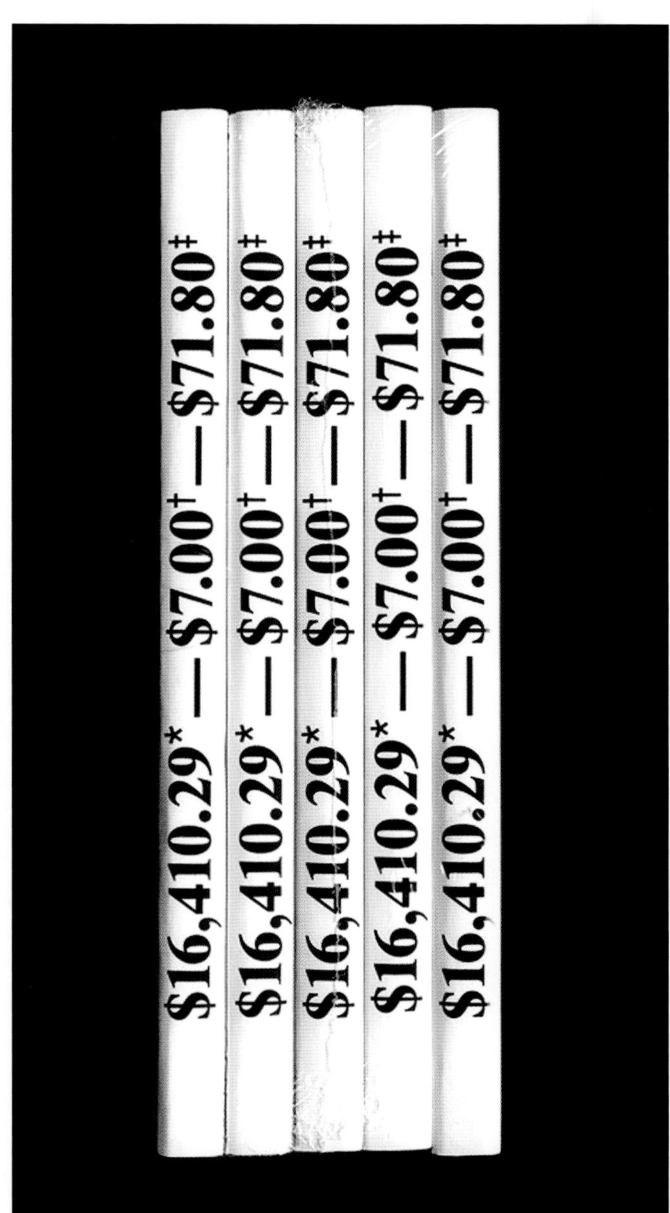

Investment Futures Strategy, Ltd.
The Book Trust Prospectus
2010 — Publication,
Corporate Identity
Design Mylinh Trieu Nguyen, Benjamin Critton, Harry Gassel, Brendan Griffiths, Zak Klauck

Investment Futures Strategies, Ltd., modeled itself after hedge funds and financial advisory firms not only conceptually, but also visually. The determined projection of seriousness and authenticity was achieved through a highly conservative identity, in which play was often inserted only in the copywriting and performance. Through extensive research of corporate financial letterhead design, Times New Roman was the typeface that embodied all of the characteristics IFS, Ltd. has as a company.

New Tab

Shri Kali
Japan

श्री कालि
आश्रम्

Information
Activities
Resources

New Tab

INFORMATION

Concepts
Biography
Blog

Shri Kali
Japan

シュリカリジャパンで伝統
的なヨガを味わう。

info@shrikali.jp
+81 80 3130 8415

中口朋子
ヨガの先生

श्री कालि
आश्रम्

Shri Kali Japan
2012 — Visual Identity
Client Shri Kali Japan
Design Twelve

"We seek to create 'the supra-mundane through the mundane'."

Shri Kali Japan is a traditional Yoga center in Osaka. It provides Yoga lessons, teacher couching and organizes Yoga retreats. It is a Japanese branch of Shri Kali Ashram, located near Galgibaga, India. Twelve was commissioned to design the visual identity and the website. Drawing the connection between the metaphysical doctrines of Shri Kali Ashram and the Gestalt psychology, we created the identity based on simple typography and reversed graphics. It is both concise and sober. With careful editing, both text and images, we seek to create 'the supra-mundane through the mundane'.

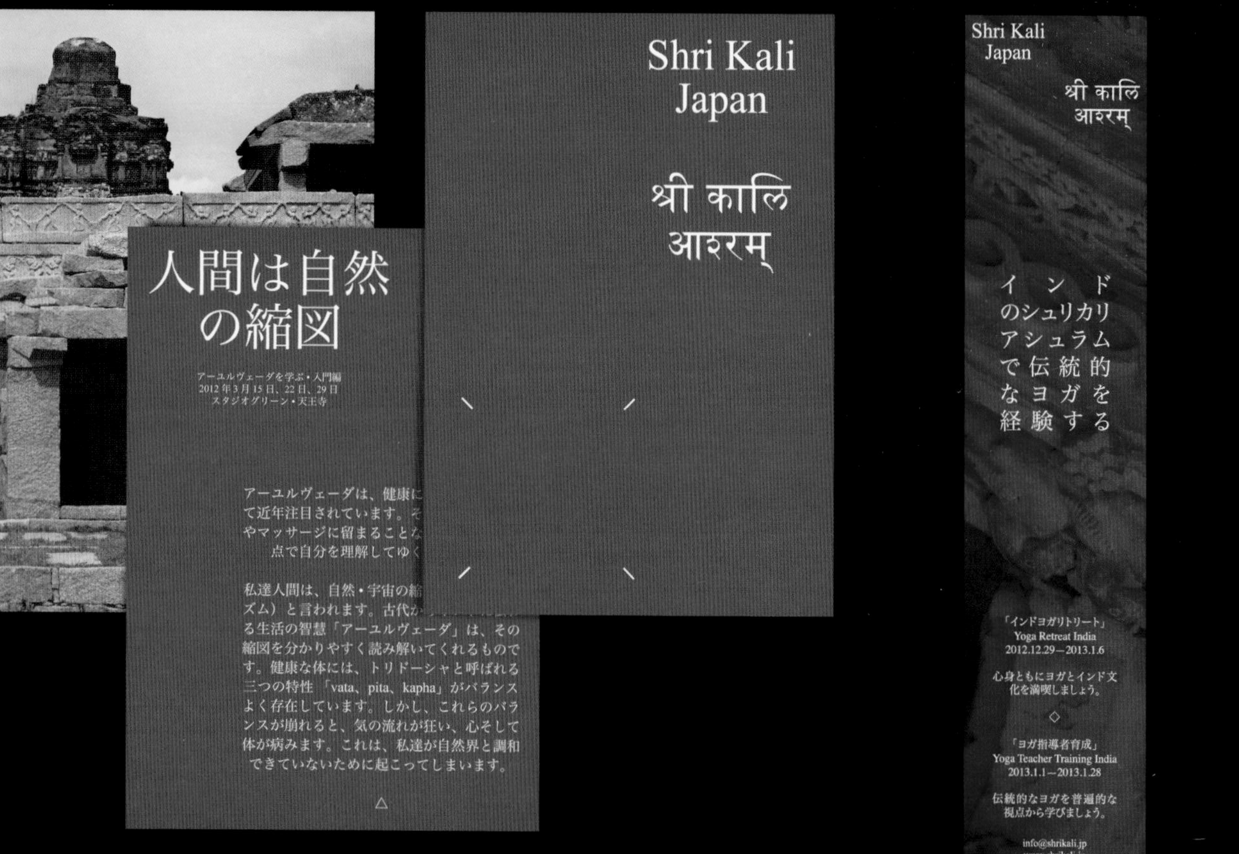
人間は自然
の縮図
アーユルヴェーダを学ぶ・入門編
2012年3月15日、22日、29日
スタジオグリーン・天王寺
アーユルヴェーダは、健康に
て近年注目されています。そ
やマッサージに留まることな
点で自分を理解してゆく
私達人間は、自然・宇宙の縮
ズム）と言われます。古代か
る生活の智慧「アーユルヴェーダ」は、その
縮図を分かりやすく読み解いてくれるもので
す。健康な体には、トリドーシャと呼ばれる
三つの特性「vata、pita、kapha」がバランス
よく存在しています。しかし、これらのバラ
ンスが崩れると、気の流れが狂い、心そして
体が病みます。これは、私達が自然界と調和
できていないために起こってしまいます。
△
Shri Kali
Japan
श्री कालि
आश्रम्
Shri Kali
Japan
श्री कालि
आश्रम्
インド
のシュリカリ
アシュラム
で伝統的
なヨガを
経験する
「インドヨガリトリート」
Yoga Retreat India
2012.12.29—2013.1.6
心身ともにヨガとインド文
化を満喫しましょう。
◇
「ヨガ指導者育成」
Yoga Teacher Training India
2013.1.1—2013.1.28
伝統的なヨガを普遍的な
視点から学びましょう。
info@shrikali.jp
www.shrikali.jp

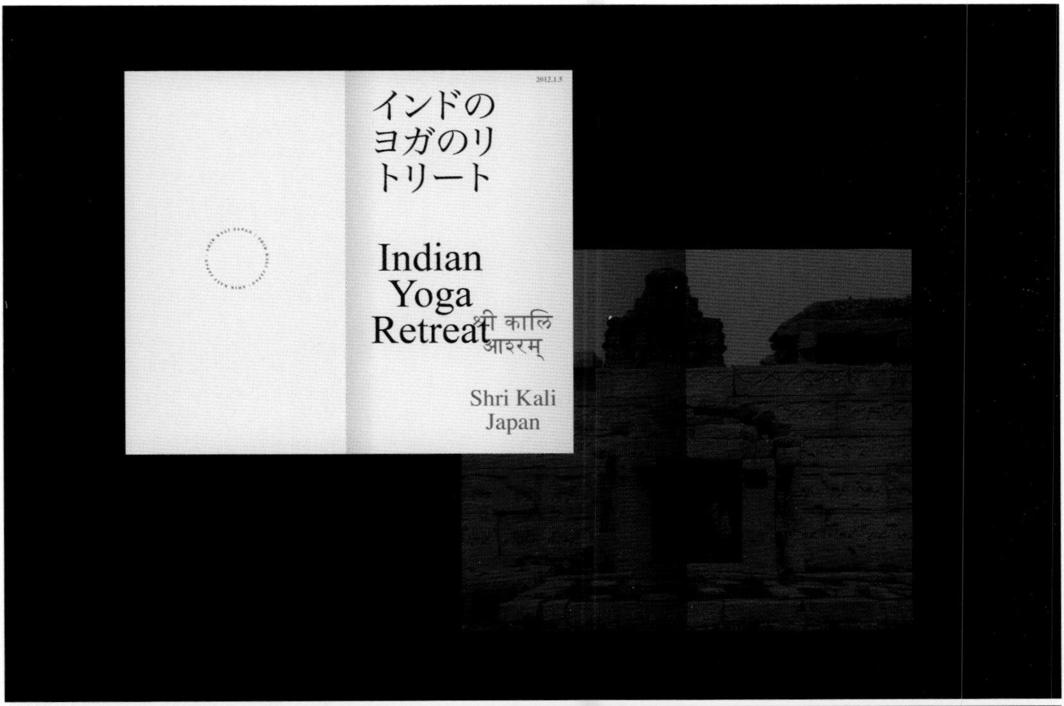

2012.1.5

インドの
ヨガのリ
トリート

Indian
Yoga
Retreat

श्री कालि
आश्रम्

Shri Kali
Japan

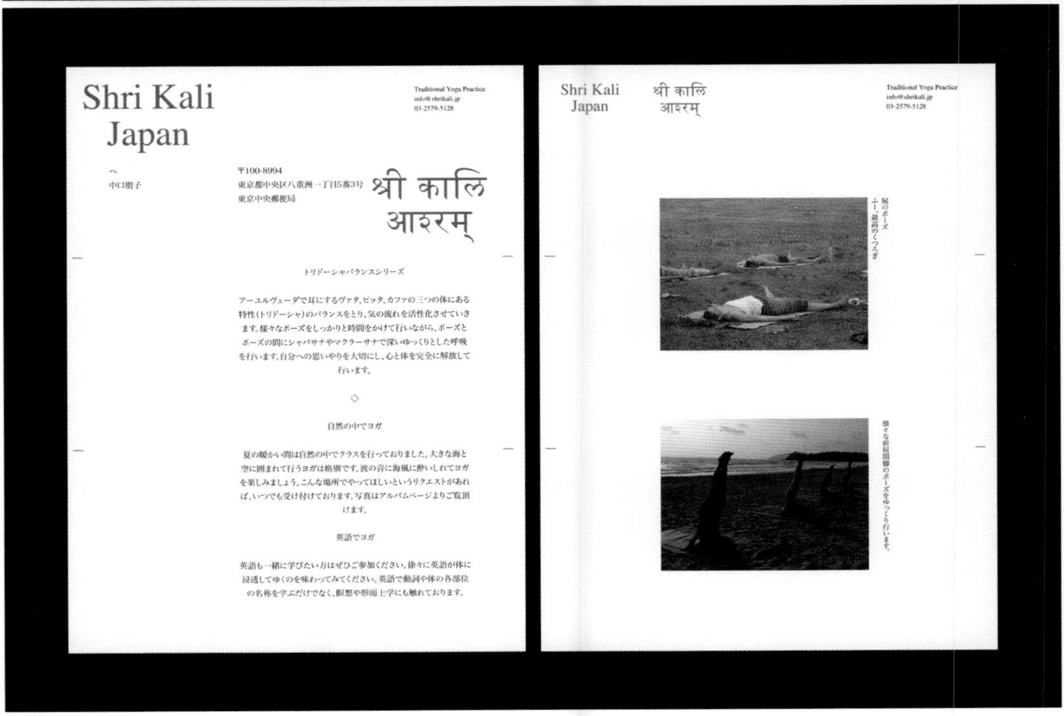

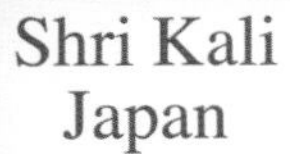

Shri Kali
Japan

Traditional Yoga Practice
info@shrikali.jp
03-2579-5128

へ
中口朋子

〒100-8994
東京都中央区八重洲一丁目5番3号
東京中央郵便局

श्री कालि
आश्रम्

トリドーシャバランスシリーズ

アーユルヴェーダで耳にするヴァタ、ピッタ、カファの三つの体にある特性(トリドーシャ)のバランスをとり、気の流れを活性化させていきます。様々なポーズをしっかりと時間をかけて行いながら、ポーズとポーズの間にシャバサナやマクラーサナで深いゆっくりとした呼吸を行います。自分への思いやりを大切にし、心と体を完全に解放して行います。

◇

自然の中でヨガ

夏の暖かい間は自然の中でクラスを行っておりました。大きな海と空に囲まれて行うヨガは格別です。波の音に海風に酔いしれてヨガを楽しみましょう。こんな場所でやってほしいというリクエストがあれば、いつでも受け付けております。写真はアルバムページよりご覧頂けます。

英語でヨガ

英語も一緒に学びたい方はぜひご参加ください。徐々に英語が体に浸透してゆくのを味わってみてください。英語で動詞や体の各部位の名称を学ぶだけでなく、瞑想や形而上学にも触れております。

Shri Kali
Japan

श्री कालि
आश्रम्

Traditional Yoga Practice
info@shrikali.jp
03-2579-5128

屍のポーズ
ふー、最高のくつろぎ

様々な前屈開脚のポーズをゆっくり行います。

We'll Die Smiling
New Objectivity EP Artwork
2012 — Vinyl Packaging
Client We'll Die Smiling
Design Catalogue

Design for the vinyl release of UK band 'We'll Die Smiling's 2012 EP 'New Objectivity'. The band creates an abrasive sound and often plays in unusual and progressive time signatures while still having references to earlier sounds and styles. We wanted to represent this in the artwork for the release so decided to take the classic typeface Times, then stretch and warp the letterforms out of place to create a harsher and more unusual version of the original.

"The serif letterforms looked especially interesting and unusual when stretched and warped."

PIG Decade — A selection of interviews,
independent photography and other goods.

Pig Decade
2012 — Magazine
Client Pig Magazine
Design Tankboys
(Lorenzo Mason,
Marco Campardo)

We redesigned the famous Italian magazine Pig and wanted to use the most basic and common typeface, Times and Helvetica, both in medium weight.

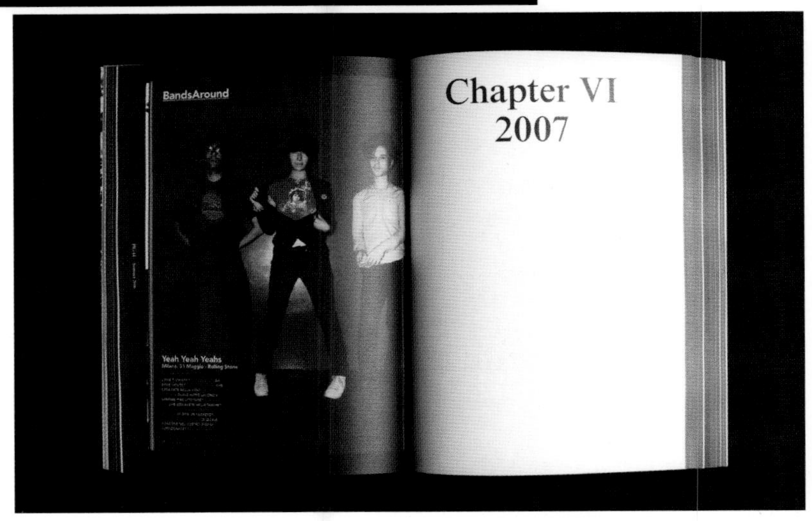

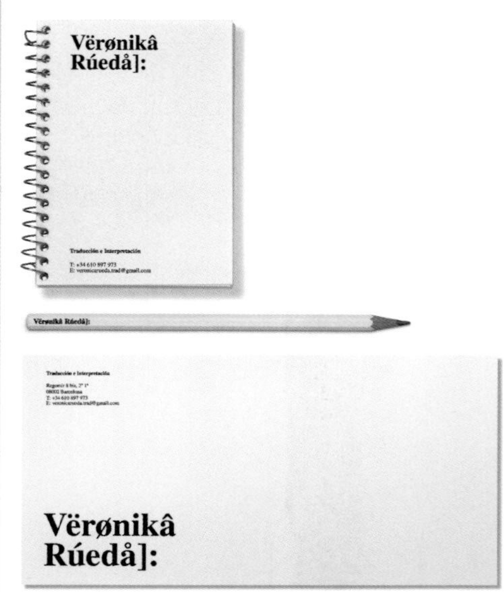

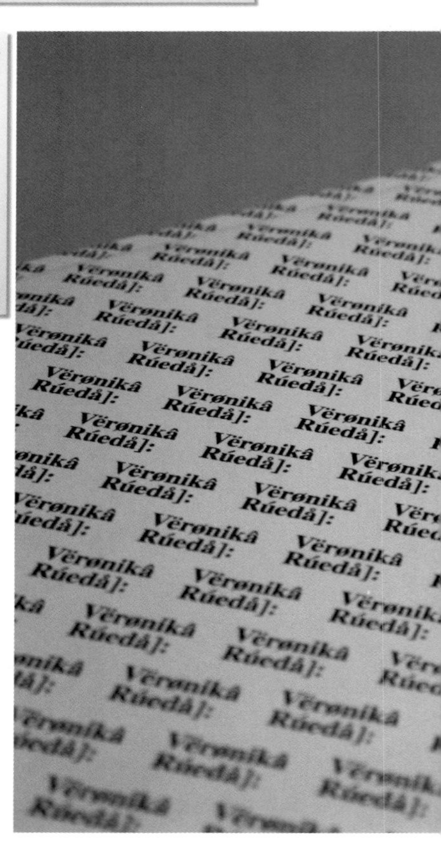

Typeface in Use
Times LT Std

"I used Times, because as a serif typeface it alludes to the literary text (the specialization of the translator), and because of the presence of a phonetic weight. Times, in addition, possesses a familiar quality, due to the fact that it has been used enough."

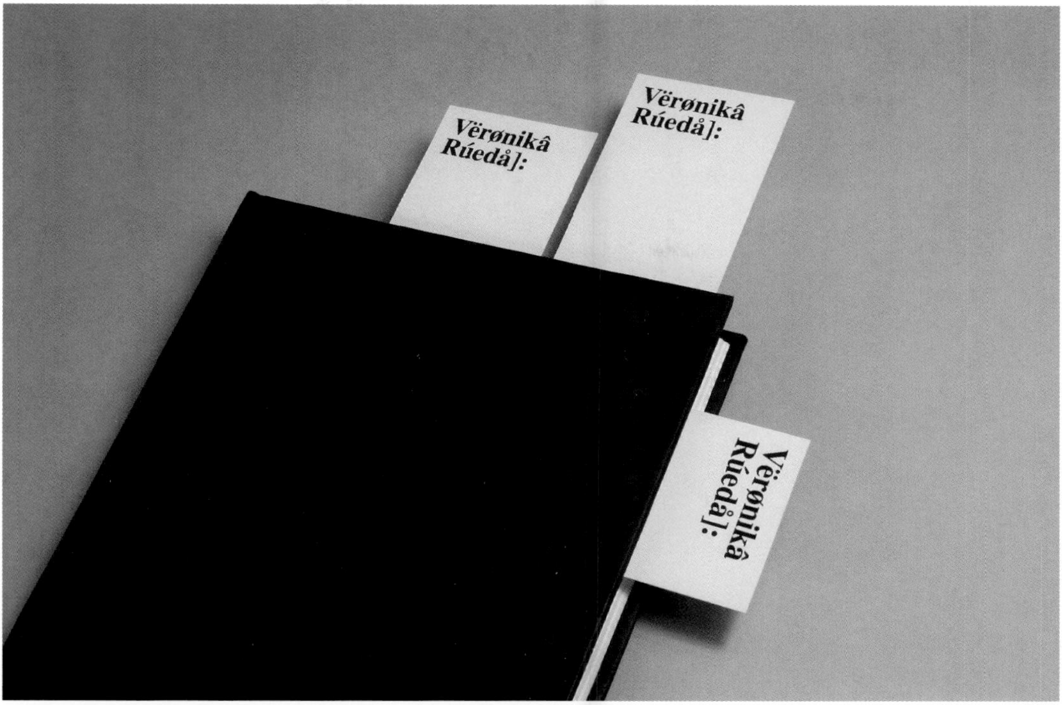

Translation
2012 — Corporate Identity
Client Verónica Rueda
Design Elio Salichs

Verónica Rueda is a translator and interpreter (focused on literary text). The use of different characters and typographic glyphs is what underlines her profession. Characters are composed in black on a white background alluding to literary world.

a

Elio Salichs' Favorite Times Letter is "a".

Litteratur
huset
STVG

Litteratur
huset
STVG

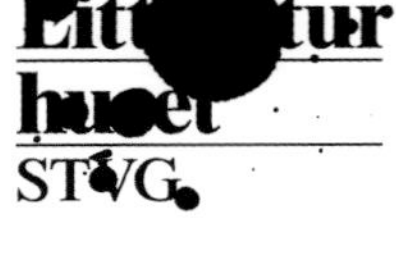

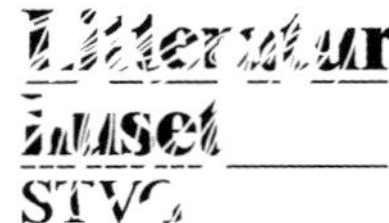

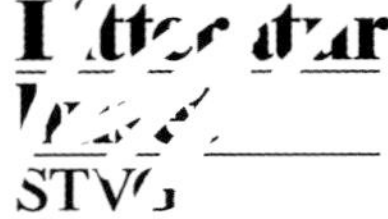

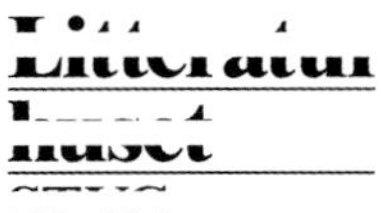

Li tur
hu
STVG

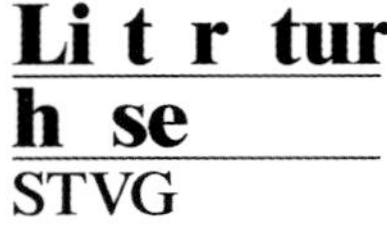

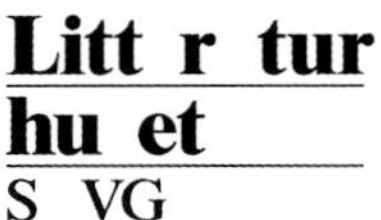

T s e a

"A visual system that offered dynamic solutions was necessary, embracing any direction the project would take, both content-wise and in its communication with the audience. Furthermore, it was clear that most of the communication material would be produced by the Litteraturhuset staff themselves, and that the visual identity had to be based on modules to be easily applied anywhere.

Regarding all the flexibility and playfulness implied, clear references to Literature were necessary. Even if Times not traditionally regarded as a suitable book design typeface, we chose it as 'the' generic [serif] typeface for representing the act of writing – often much more used during the writing process itself (e.g. the author writing the script in MS Word), with all its iterations, feedback from readers, before publishing a final conclusion of the text. [And, of course, setting a title in Times Extra Bold is a humble reminiscence to Willy Fleckhaus' Suhrkamp taschenbuch covers]. Another reason was the temptation to brand by means of an everyday and everyone's object like the typeface Times."*

Typeface in Use
Times LT Std

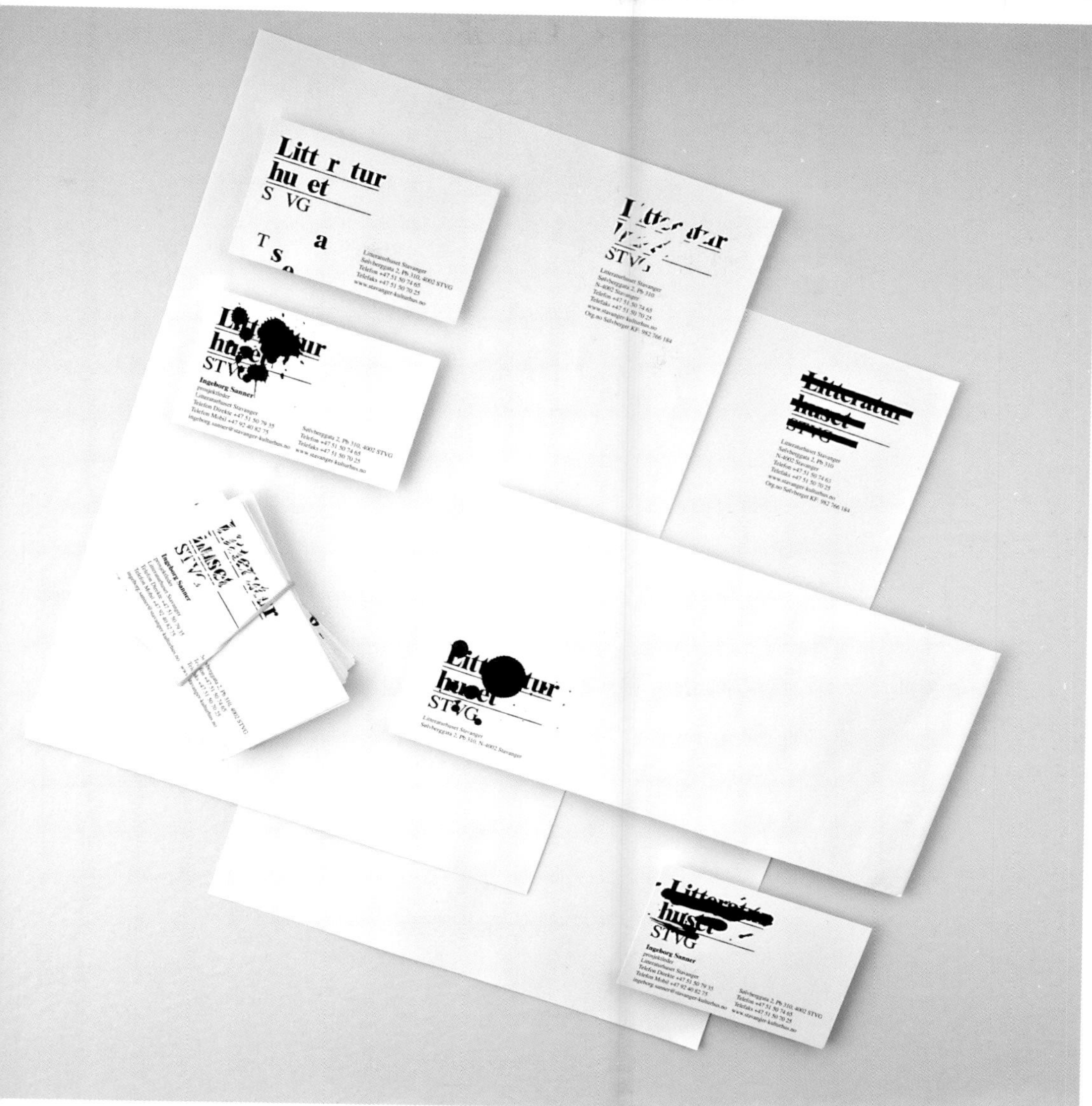

Litteraturhuset STVG
2010 — Visual Identity
Client House of Literature Stavanger
Design Fasett
(Trond Fernblad, Benjamin Hickethier)

At the starting point of the process, there was not much more than Stavanger municipality's plan to establish a House of Literature (Litteraturhuset). What it should be filled with, where it should be sited and what exactly it should be, had yet to be decided.

Litteraturhuset's identity will be able to grow and develop with the project itself by design. Just as with the Litteraturhuset, some parameters are defined, some are not — users/readers are invited to join, give their input and build on it. The expression varies already with a continuously expanding collection of 12 variations of the logo itself.

Since the launch of the Litteraturhuset, it has become a thriving focal point for the mediation of factual and literary matter, debate, dialog, literature activities for children and exciting lectures and interviews, amongst many other things, and an important partner for Kapittel, Stavanger's acquainted international festival of Literature and Freedom of Speech (which we are also honored having designed the visual identity program for).

N

Chris Steurer's Favorite Times Letter is "N".

"When designing in black and white only, Times New Roman is the first choice for me. It seems to be the most invisible serif typeface. Therefore i love to make it visible (without becoming too pretentious)!"

Typeface in Use
Times New Roman Italic, Times New Roman Bold,
Times New Roman Bold Italic, Berthold Akzidenz Grotesk Bold

WIR KOeNNEN AUCH ANDERS
2011 — Brochure, Posters
Client SchönSchräg Hairdressers, Wiesbaden
Design Chris Steurer
Photography Christiane Haid (brochure), Simon Hegenberg (poster)

Tattoos and piercings make hairstylist Christian look like a so-called tough guy. He assigned the image campaign WE CAN DO IT DIFFERENTLY because he wanted to show how focused he is on professional hairstyling and on assisting everyday-people with their hairstyle — no matter how old they are. Despite his tough guy look, Christian has a wide range of clients aged from 15 to 75, as this little mag shows.

Some months later the campaign was refreshed with a poster series which uses a more radical photographic speech.

to regulate the content of television, radio and the written press, the blocking of protests, the keeping of political and military information private on grounds of national security (while convincing people that the government is acting in their interests) and other forms of limiting and filtering information are all proof of an effectively implemented censorship.

What are the limits and means of self-expression and freedom of speech, and the new forms of censorship/self-censorship today? How effective is communication through printed matter in a world dominated by the internet and the popularity of social networks?

Publishing as a means of self-expression and samizdat as a one of its forms, born in specific oppressive conditions, might shed some new light on the meaning of self-publishing today, on its present forms and challenges. The theoretical texts in this publication provide an overview of the genesis of samizdat as a common phenomenon in the Eastern bloc countries, a survey of self-publishing in Poland and a perspective on resistance and the new forms of protest in Russia. On the one hand, this project has brought socio-political practice into discussion through the holding of debates and seminars, while, on the other hand, it contained a practical component of experimentation with printed matter. The workshop created a framework within which the participants could present their own case studies related to self-publishing and also worked as a mechanism of editorial aggregation for this context. It comprises a series of heterogeneous approaches originating from different disciplines and cultural practices, thus extending and giving substance to the issues incorporated by self-publishing: self-organization, self-archiving, publishing as a tool of legitimizing and establishing; editing as a process of defining and revealing; distribution as an instrument of communication, publishing that lead to repression, publishing to fight for freedom, the periphery of self-publishing; the economics of attention as a key factor in success; linguistics and censorship through translation with reference to the dominance of the English language.

The structure of this publication is envisioned as a succession of visual essays, as thoughts in printed form, interconnected through footnotes and assembled as a collective discourse. This is just the first stage in a series of different events to be held in the future under the umbrella of the Centre for Visual Introspection.

22

to regulate the content of television, radio and the written press, the blocking of protests, the keeping of political and military information private on grounds of national security (while convincing people that the government is acting in their interests) and other forms of limiting and filtering information are all proof of an effectively implemented censorship.

What are the limits and means of self-expression and freedom of speech, and the new forms of censorship/self-censorship today? How effective is communication through printed matter in a world dominated by the internet and the popularity of social networks?

Publishing as a means of self-expression and samizdat as a one of its forms, born in specific oppressive conditions, might shed some new light on the meaning of self-publishing today, on its present forms and challenges. The theoretical texts in this publication provide an overview of the genesis of samizdat as a common phenomenon in the Eastern bloc countries, a survey of self-publishing in Poland and a perspective on resistance and the new forms of protest in Russia. On the one hand, this project has brought socio-political practice into discussion through the holding of debates and seminars, while, on the other hand, it contained a practical component of experimentation with printed matter. The workshop created a framework within which the participants could present their own case studies related to self-publishing and also worked as a mechanism of editorial aggregation for this context. It comprises a series of heterogeneous approaches originating from different disciplines and cultural practices, thus extending and giving substance to the issues incorporated by self-publishing: self-organization, self-archiving, publishing as a tool of legitimizing and establishing; editing as a process of defining and revealing; distribution as an instrument of communication, publishing that lead to repression, publishing to fight for freedom, the periphery of self-publishing; the economics of attention as a key factor in success; linguistics and censorship through translation with reference to the dominance of the English language.

The structure of this publication is envisioned as a succession of visual essays, as thoughts in printed form, interconnected through footnotes and assembled as a collective discourse. This is just the first stage in a series of different events to be held in the future under the umbrella of the Centre for Visual Introspection.

22

EDITORIAL

This publication is released within the framework of the project "Hard Edit—Self-publishing in Times of Freedom and Repression", which consisted of a series of lectures by Vasile Ernu [RO], Lia Perjovschi [RO], Piotr Rypson [PL], Olga Zaslavskaya [RU] and a practical workshop, held between 18 and 24 April 2011 at the Centre for Visual Introspection in Bucharest, by Marco Balesteros and Sofia Gonçalves [PT], with the contribution of Renata Catambas [PT/NL], Rafaela Dražić [CRO], Eleonora Farina [IT/DE], Ward Heirwegh [BE], Tzortzis Rallis [GR/UK], Katarina Šević [SRB/HU], Golie Talaie [IR/NL] and Paul Wiersbinski [DE].

The background to this project is given by the "interrupted history" of self-publishing in Romania, an area still insufficiently acknowledged and researched. The avant-garde literary tradition (*Contimporanul*, *Punct*, *Integral*, *Unu*, *Urmuz*, *Alge*), to which artists and poets contributed (Tristan Tzara, Ilarie Voronca, Ion Vinea, Urmuz, Marcel Iancu), created a background for the development of later clandestine publication, when it was interrupted during the totalitarian political regime. Under the Ceaușescu dictatorship, the ideologically imposed state regulation of the cultural and artistic realm was extremely harsh, such that the production of independent publications took pace only in closed circles or artists' studios. Authentic forms of dissidence existed in the form of a few samizdat publications in Hungarian during the 1980s – *Ellenpontok* (Counterpoints) in Oradea and *Kiáltó Szó* (Shouting word), in Cluj – but also individual practices (Ana Blandiana, Doina Cornea, Radu Filipescu, Vasile Paraschiv, Paul Goma and the artist Ion Grigorescu to name but a few); the launch of the unofficial newspaper *Romania* was planned for 1989, but its founders (Mihai Creangă, Petre Mihai Băcanu, Anton Uncu and Ștefan Niculescu Maier) were unable to distribute after having been arrested by Romania's secret services. Self--publishing began to re-appear more dynamically in the early 1990s, during the times of "freedom". Today, ideological censorship has been replaced by new constraints. On a global level, almost everything is based on economics and censorship is just as likely to be the result of market forces. In theory, the internet provides a constant flow of information on basically anything imaginable; however, the current system has its subtle, in-built mechanisms for suppressing freedom of expression that are as powerful as those of past centuries. The control of the news we get through the mass media, the passing of laws

3

EDITORIAL 3
[DE] Paul WIERSBINSKI 4
[BE] Ward HEIRWEGH 6
[IT/DE] Elenora FARINA 8
[PT/NL] Renata CATAMBAS 10
LECTURES:
[RO] Lia PERJOVSCHI 11
[RU/HU] Olga ZASLAVSKAYA 11
[PL] Piotr RYPSON 12
[RU] Vasile ERNU 12
[SRB/HU] Katarina ŠEVIĆ 14
[CRO] Rafaela DRAŽIĆ 16
[IR/NL] Golie TALAIE 18
[GR/UK] Tzortzis RALLIS 20

Hard Edit—Edit Hard
Self-Publishing in Times of Freedom and Repression
2011 — Newspaper, Workshop
Client Centre for Visual Introspection, Bucharest, Romania (I.c.w. Sofia Gonçalves)
Design Letra (Marco Balesteros)

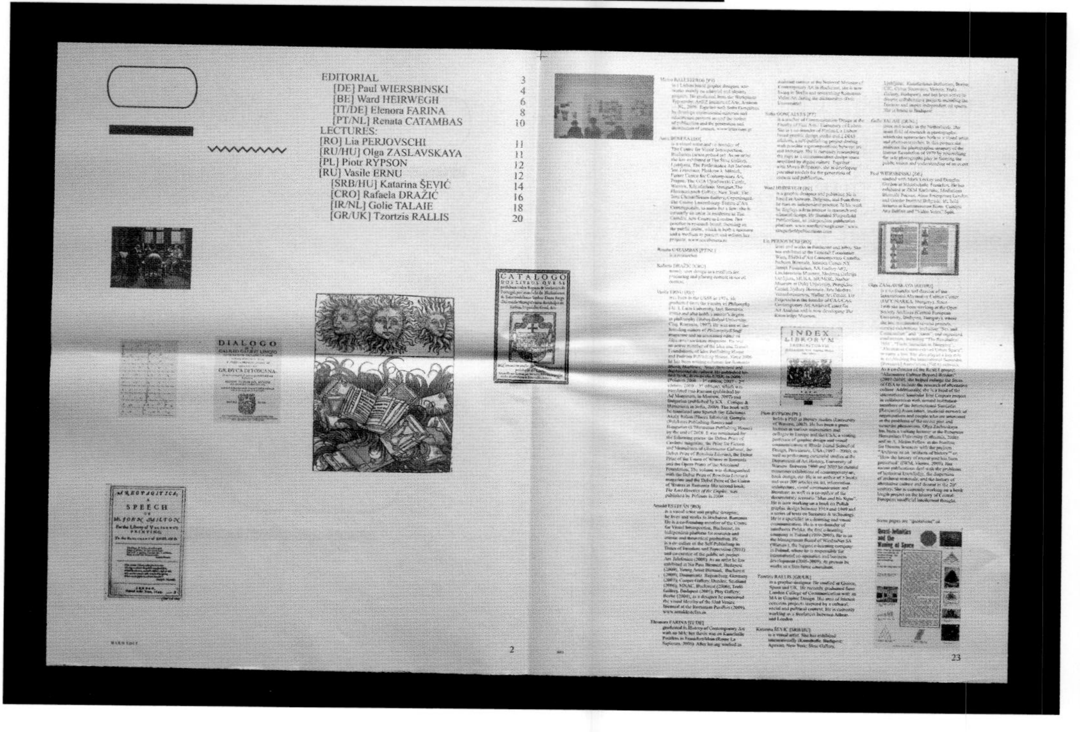

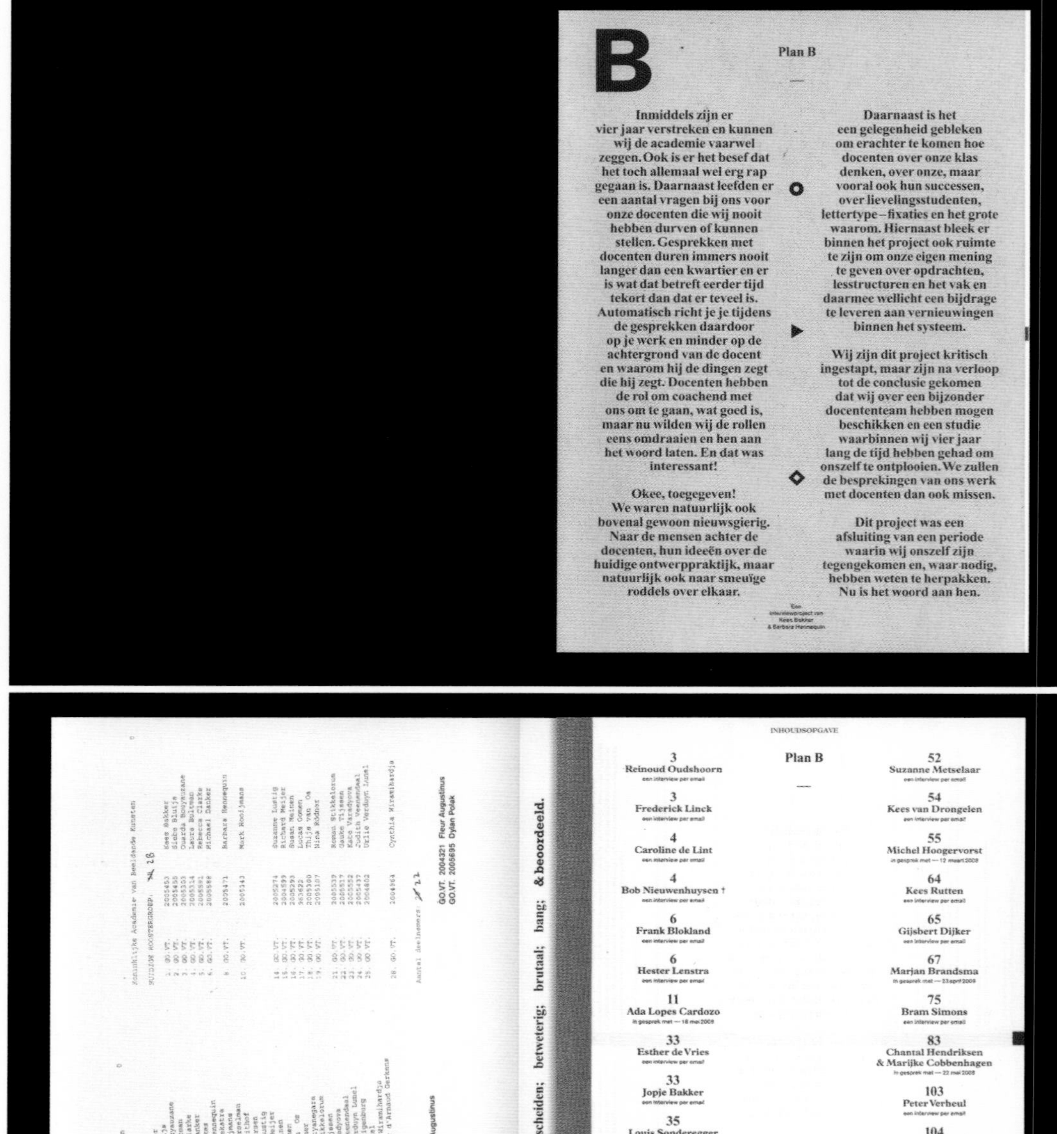

B

Plan B

—

Inmiddels zijn er vier jaar verstreken en kunnen wij de academie vaarwel zeggen. Ook is er het besef dat het toch allemaal wel erg rap gegaan is. Daarnaast leefden er een aantal vragen bij ons voor onze docenten die wij nooit hebben durven of kunnen stellen. Gesprekken met docenten duren immers nooit langer dan een kwartier en er is wat dat betreft eerder tijd tekort dan dat er teveel is. Automatisch richt je je tijdens de gesprekken daardoor op je werk en minder op de achtergrond van de docent en waarom hij de dingen zegt die hij zegt. Docenten hebben de rol om coachend met ons om te gaan, wat goed is, maar nu wilden wij de rollen eens omdraaien en hen aan het woord laten. En dat was interessant!

Okee, toegegeven! We waren natuurlijk ook bovenal gewoon nieuwsgierig. Naar de mensen achter de docenten, hun ideeën over de huidige ontwerppraktijk, maar natuurlijk ook naar smeuïge roddels over elkaar.

Daarnaast is het een gelegenheid gebleken om erachter te komen hoe docenten over onze klas denken, over onze, maar vooral ook hun successen, over lievelingsstudenten, lettertype-fixaties en het grote waarom. Hiernaast bleek er binnen het project ook ruimte te zijn om onze eigen mening te geven over opdrachten, lesstructuren en het vak en daarmee wellicht een bijdrage te leveren aan vernieuwingen binnen het systeem.

Wij zijn dit project kritisch ingestapt, maar zijn na verloop tot de conclusie gekomen dat wij over een bijzonder docententeam hebben mogen beschikken en een studie waarbinnen wij vier jaar lang de tijd hebben gehad om onszelf te ontplooien. We zullen de besprekingen van ons werk met docenten dan ook missen.

Dit project was een afsluiting van een periode waarin wij onszelf zijn tegengekomen en, waar nodig, hebben weten te herpakken. Nu is het woord aan hen.

Een interviewproject van Kees Bakker & Barbara Hennequin

b; beter; boiend; bescheiden; betweterig; brutaal; bang; & beoordeeld.

INHOUDSOPGAVE

Plan B

—

1

Typeface in Use
Times New Roman, Akzidenz Grotesk BE, Rockwell, Plantin

"We were seeking for a range of typefaces that could reflect the process of going through design education.

NOOT

Plan B

—

Oorspronkelijk zijn wij dit project gestart als extra eindexamenproject. Het organiseren, het afnemen van de interviews, het redigeren van de teksten en niet te vergeten het ontwerp van dit boek bleek al gauw van een dergelijke omvang te zijn, dat wij het project over ons eindexamen heen hebben getrokken.

Want wij wilden dit project natuurlijk niet afraffelen! Om Jan Willem Stas te citeren: "Slordige mensen zijn echt verschrikkelijk."

K&B

PLAN B

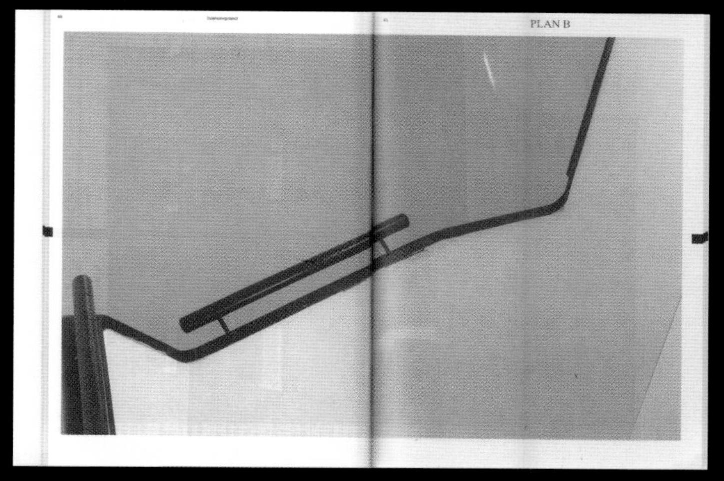

PLAN B

Beste Gijsbert Dijker,

Voor één van onze (eindexamen)projecten maken wij, Kees & Barbara, samen een boek met als overkoepelend thema het afsluiten van vier jaar studeren aan de KABK van onze klas. Hiervoor interviewen we alle docenten van wie we tijdens deze vier jaar les hebben gehad. Het zou fijn zijn als ook jij onze vragen zou willen invullen. Dit neemt zo ongeveer

Plan B
2010 — Publication
Design Kees Bakker,
Barbara Hennequin

Plan B is a Kees Bakker & Barbara Hennequin book project, which includes 28 interviews with their former proffesors (Gert Dumbar, Hendriksen & Cobbenhagen, Jost Rossum, to name a few) from the Graphic Design department of the Royal Academy of Art, the Hague. The professors were asked to expose their vision on graphic design of today, about their own work, their successes and setbacks, the influence of teaching and the reflection of it on their own work, their favorite student(s), interests, ideals, favorite typeface, and so on.

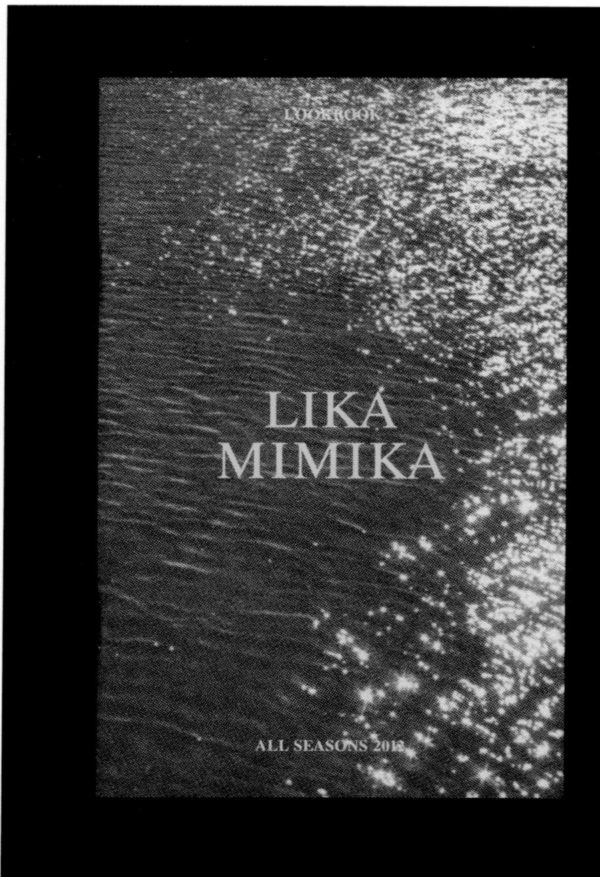

Lika Mimika
2012 — Lookbook
Client Lika Mimika
Design Doeller & Satter

Lookbook 2012 for the fashion company Lika Mimika.

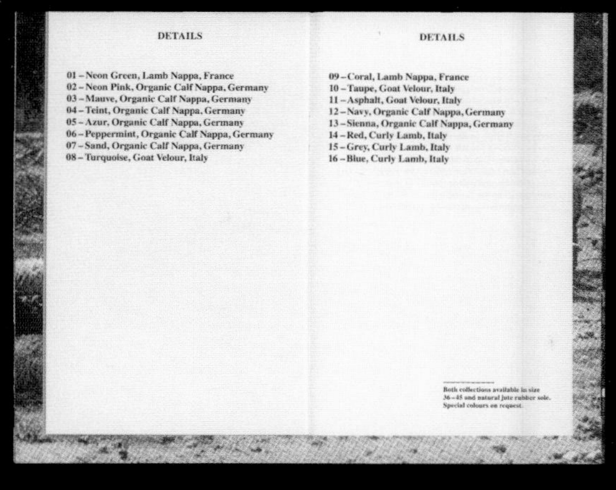
DETAILS
01 – Neon Green, Lamb Nappa, France
02 – Neon Pink, Organic Calf Nappa, Germany
03 – Mauve, Organic Calf Nappa, Germany
04 – Teint, Organic Calf Nappa, Germany
05 – Azur, Organic Calf Nappa, Germany
06 – Peppermint, Organic Calf Nappa, Germany
07 – Sand, Organic Calf Nappa, Germany
08 – Turquoise, Goat Velour, Italy
DETAILS
09 – Coral, Lamb Nappa, France
10 – Taupe, Goat Velour, Italy
11 – Asphalt, Goat Velour, Italy
12 – Navy, Organic Calf Nappa, Germany
13 – Sienna, Organic Calf Nappa, Germany
14 – Red, Curly Lamb, Italy
15 – Grey, Curly Lamb, Italy
16 – Blue, Curly Lamb, Italy
Both collections available in size
36 – 45 and natural jute rubber sole.
Special colours on request.

LIKA MIMIKA
Concept and Design: Doeller & Satter
Product Shots: Katrin Binner

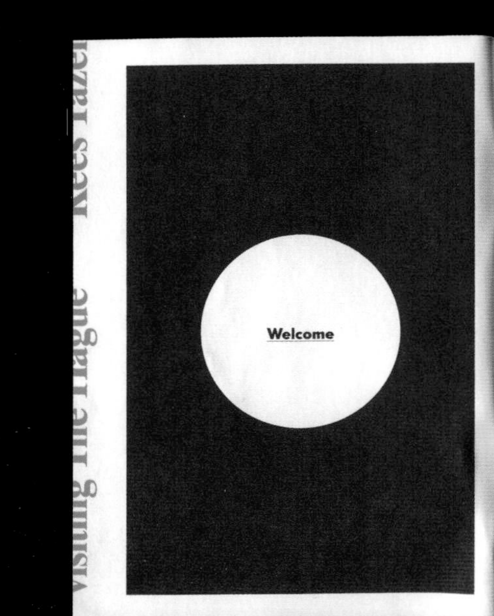

3

This year, it is sixty years ago that **Pierre Schaeffer** launched a new approach to music, which he called **Musique Concrète**. At the same time, it is fifty years ago that the **Groupe de Recherches Musicales** was founded. Therefore, **the Institute of Sonology of the Royal Conservatory** decided to organise a three-day festival for which the GRM loudspeaker orchestra — **the Acousmonium** — will be transported from Paris to the Arnold Schoenberg Hall. A program with four concerts will give an overview of early and more recent works from the GRM studio. In a fifth concert, the results of a workshop with six Sonology students under guidance of the GRM technicians and composers will be presented.

The difference between the two main streams of post-war electronic music is often explained by stating that initially, the **Cologne** composers would exclusively use electronically generated sound material, whereas the **Paris** composers would exclusively use sounds recorded with a microphone. **Stockhausen** then would be the first to break with the Cologne dogmas by using the recordings of a boy's voice in his **Gesang der Junglinge** (*1955–1956*).

Acousmonium visiting The Hague
Preface Kees Tazelaar

Typeface in Use
Times Ten

"I like the 'bold formality' of it."

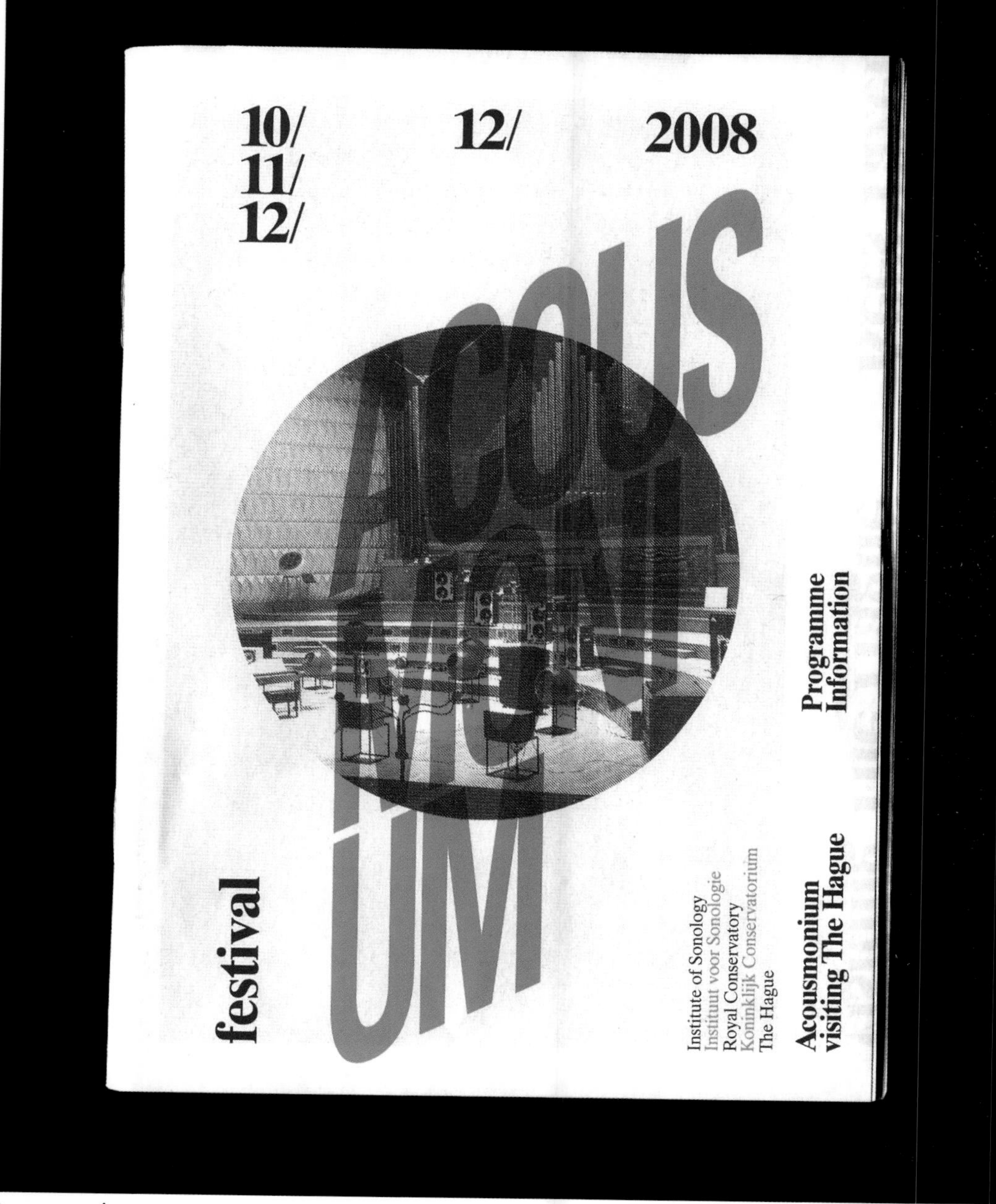

Acousmonium
2008 — Program Booklet, Flyer
Client The Royal Conservatoire of The Hague, the Netherlands
Design Rob van den Nieuwenhuizen

This program booklet was designed for a very special concert series of GRM's Acousmonium orchestra. The Acousmonium is the sound diffusion system designed in 1974 by Francois Bayle and consists of 80 loudspeakers of differing size and shape, and was designed for tape playback.

Concerts

13

Concert 1

Edgard Varèse
Christian Zanési
Luc Ferrari
Denis Dufour

Sound projection: Christian Zanési

Concert 1
Wednesday December 10th

Acousmonium
visiting The Hague

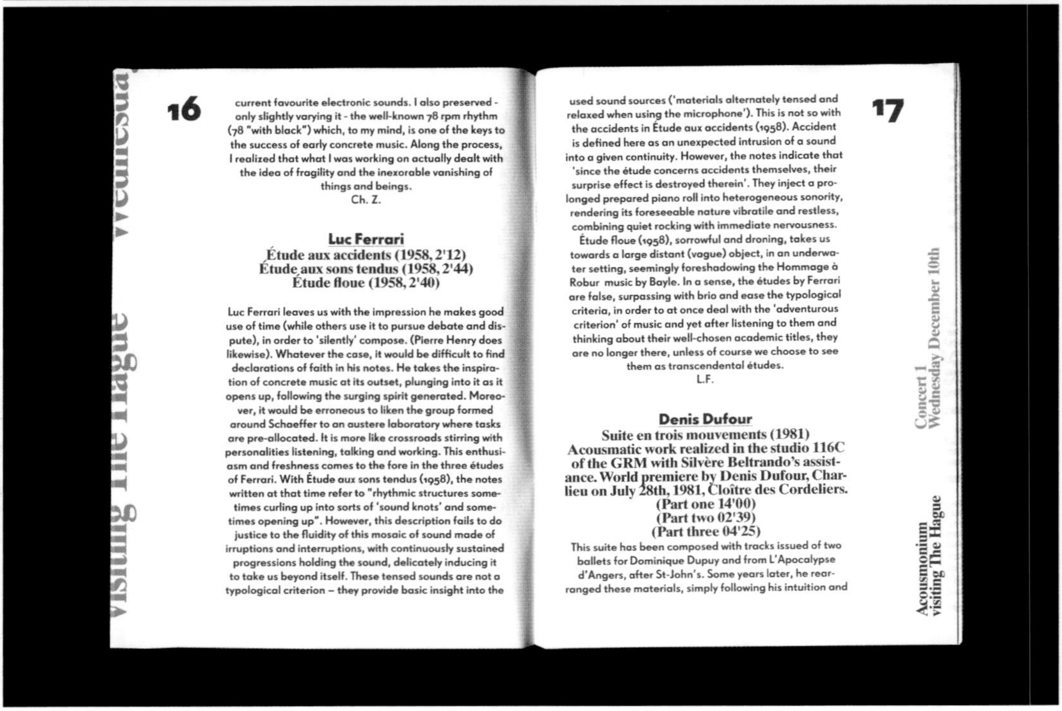

16

current favourite electronic sounds. I also preserved - only slightly varying it - the well-known 78 rpm rhythm (78 "with black") which, to my mind, is one of the keys to the success of early concrete music. Along the process, I realized that what I was working on actually dealt with the idea of fragility and the inexorable vanishing of things and beings.

Ch. Z.

Luc Ferrari

Étude aux accidents (1958, 2'12)
Étude aux sons tendus (1958, 2'44)
Étude floue (1958, 2'40)

Luc Ferrari leaves us with the impression he makes good use of time (while others use it to pursue debate and dispute), in order to 'silently' compose. (Pierre Henry does likewise). Whatever the case, it would be difficult to find declarations of faith in his notes. He takes the inspiration of concrete music at its outset, plunging into it as it opens up, following the surging spirit generated. Moreover, it would be erroneous to liken the group formed around Schaeffer to an austere laboratory where tasks are pre-allocated. It is more like crossroads stirring with personalities listening, talking and working. This enthusiasm and freshness comes to the fore in the three études of Ferrari. With Étude aux sons tendus (1958), the notes written at that time refer to "rhythmic structures sometimes curling up into sorts of 'sound knots' and sometimes opening up". However, this description fails to do justice to the fluidity of this mosaic of sound made of irruptions and interruptions, with continuously sustained progressions holding the sound, delicately inducing it to take us beyond itself. These tensed sounds are not a typological criterion – they provide basic insight into the

17

used sound sources ('materials alternately tensed and relaxed when using the microphone'). This is not so with the accidents in Étude aux accidents (1958). Accident is defined here as an unexpected intrusion of a sound into a given continuity. However, the notes indicate that 'since the étude concerns accidents themselves, their surprise effect is destroyed therein'. They inject a prolonged prepared piano roll into heterogeneous sonority, rendering its foreseeable nature vibratile and restless, combining quiet rocking with immediate nervousness. Étude floue (1958), sorrowful and droning, takes us towards a large distant (vague) object, in an underwater setting, seemingly foreshadowing the Hommage à Robur music by Bayle. In a sense, the études by Ferrari are false, surpassing with brio and ease the typological criteria, in order to at once deal with the 'adventurous criterion' of music and yet after listening to them and thinking about their well-chosen academic titles, they are no longer there, unless of course we choose to see them as transcendental études.

L.F.

Denis Dufour

Suite en trois mouvements (1981)
Acousmatic work realized in the studio 116C of the GRM with Silvère Beltrando's assistance. World premiere by Denis Dufour, Charlieu on July 28th, 1981, Cloître des Cordeliers.
(Part one 14'00)
(Part two 02'39)
(Part three 04'25)

This suite has been composed with tracks issued of two ballets for Dominique Dupuy and from L'Apocalypse d'Angers, after St-John's. Some years later, he rearranged these materials, simply following his intuition and

Concert 1
Wednesday December 10th

Acousmonium
visiting The Hague

Concert 4

Presentation of the results of the Acous-monium workshop for students of the Institute of Sonology

Concert 5

Edgard Varèse Pierre Schaeffer Michel Redolfi François Donato Daniel Teruggi

Sound projection: Daniel Teruggi

natural sound sources and computer-based studio transformations. He was first prize winner in the 1996 Stockholm Electronic Arts Award (for his work Inner) and in the 2007 Bourges Competition (for Ricordiamo Forlì) and has been a visiting composer at several institutions in Europe and North and South America. Two solo discs of his music are available on the Montréal-based Empreintes Digitales label: La Limited du bruit and Lieu-temps. *http://www.electrocd.com/en/bio/young_jo/discog/*

Pierre Henry

(Paris, 1927)

He studied music since he was 7. He studied at the High Conservatory of Music in Paris from 1937 to 1947, mainly with Olivier Messiaen, Félix Passerone and Nadia Boulanger.
He joined Pierre Schaeffer at the **Groupe de Musique Concrète** in 1949. Together they composed **Symphonie pour un homme seul** (1950) and **Orphée 51**.
His personal works from that time (all musique concrète) include: **Le microphone bien tempéré** (1950 – 1951), **Le voile d'Orphée** (1953). In 1958, he left the Radio and founded his own studio (1958 – 1982) – the first private studio devoted to electro-acoustic music. Here he composed music for many films, ballets and for publicity.
Maurice Béjart created a version of the **Symphonie pour un homme seul** in 1955 and was to create 15 other ballets with Pierre Henry.
Other collaborations with choreographers included Georges Balanchine, Carolyn Carlson, Merce Cunningham, Alwin Nikolaïs, and Maguy Marin.
Numerous concerts with his works have been performed all around the world.
As an absolute innovator in the domain of aesthetics and sound and pioneer of a new musical freedom, Pierre Henry has opened through the use of his technological researches the way to many other musical universes.
Since 1995 all contemporary generations of music homage Pierre Henry for the revolutionary inventions he has originated, innovations all reinvested in today's electronica music.
Pierre Henry's modernity is always there.
Son/RE, his Studio, is financed by the French Government.

Above all he is known as the father of musique concrète, but he was also an excellent writer, a radio pioneer and veteran and the founder and director of many services, including the Research Department at the ORTF, which he directed from 1960 to 1975.
Finally, he was a thinker and researcher, devoting a great deal of thought to audiovisual techniques (**Machines à communiquer**) and, above all, to music.

Michel Redolfi

(*Marseille, 1951*)

Michel Redolfi developed his sound creations in the United States where, at of the age of 21, he was a guest resident of important electronic music studios at the University of Wisconsin and Dartmouth College. During this period, he participated in the advent of the first digital synthesizers.
In 1981, he presented **Sonic Waters in the Pacific**, the first concert in history where music was broadcast **underwater** for a large audience floating or submerged in diving suits. The immediate recognition of this new form of listening led to other projects in the United States, Europe and Australia.
Michel Redolfi was the director of the **International Music Research Centre** (CIRM) in Nice from 1987 to 1998, as well as the head of the **MANCA Contemporary Music Festival** in the same city.
In 2003, he founded **Audionaute**, an independent production studio and a publishing label focused on underwater music and related innovative systems.
Michel Redolfi was awarded the prestigious Ars Electronica Prize in 1996. In 2006, he was nominated for the Music Golden Lion at the Venice Biennale, where he performed one of his major underwater concerts **The Liquid City**. In 2008, Walt Disney Pictures commissioned him for two underwater music concerts in Monte Carlo (sea and pool) to launch the European press premiere of **The Little Mermaid 3**.

François Donato

(*1963*)

Donato was self-taught until the age of twenty, then studied at the University of Pau in France. There he discovered and practiced the "Concrete music". He joined the GRM in 1991

LBD – Little Black Dress

52

Josefstrasse 45
8005 Zürich

As far as Eliane Diethelm and Joanna Skoczylas are concerned, the little black dress, although a true masterpiece, need be neither black nor little, but may also be colourful and worn floor-length, feminine à la Breakfast at Tiffany's or glamorous enough for a dinner party, and elegant for just about every occasion in between.

Das kleine Schwarze ist grosse Kunst und muss – frei nach Eliane Diethelm und Joanna Skoczylas – nicht zwingend schwarz oder kurz sein. Es kann auch in Farbe oder bodenlang getragen werden. Feminin zum Frühstück bei Tiffany's, glamourös zur Dinnerparty und elegant für überall zwischendurch.

T 043 540 16 70
www.littleblackdress.ch
mail@littleblackdress.ch
Di–Fr/Tue–Fri 12.00–18.30
Sa 11.00–17.00
VBZ/Public transport:
Museum für Gestaltung 4, 13, 17
Röntgenstrasse 32

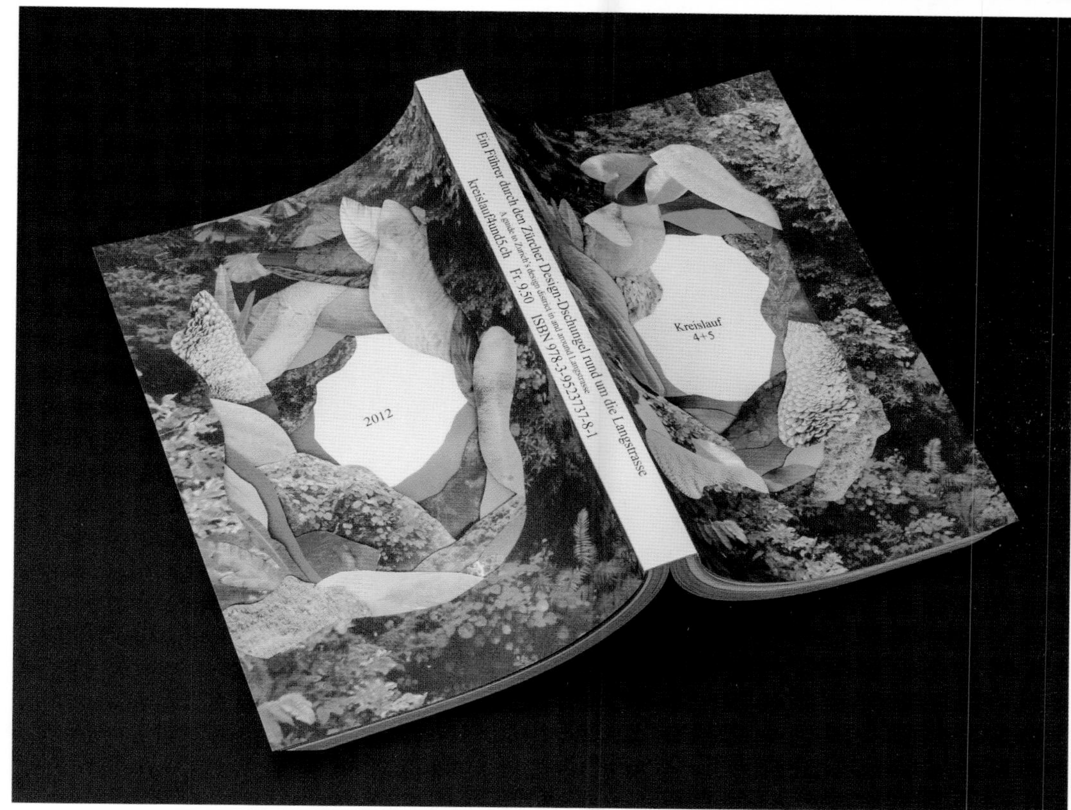

Kreislauf 4+5
2012 — Editorial Design
Client René Grüninger PR
Design Raffinerie AG für Gestaltung

Here in Zurich, on either of Langstrasse, lies the real heart of the city, the pulsating center that drives its creativity, its ideas, its flair for design and its originality. The area's culture is protean, and is acted out against a cosmopolitan backdrop that has retained its local color. Home to some of the city's most exciting and original shops and stores, it has diversity, a style and a personality that set it clearly apart from anything you may associate with other city centers and shopping malls. Kreislauf 4+5 is a platform where over 80 boutiques and studios in and around Langstrasse are able to draw deserved attention to themselves. The new, lavishly illustrated Kreislauf 4+5 guide is an introduction to the area on either side of Langstrasse with around 250 pages featuring maps of the districts, editorial contributions and portraits of all the stores involved.

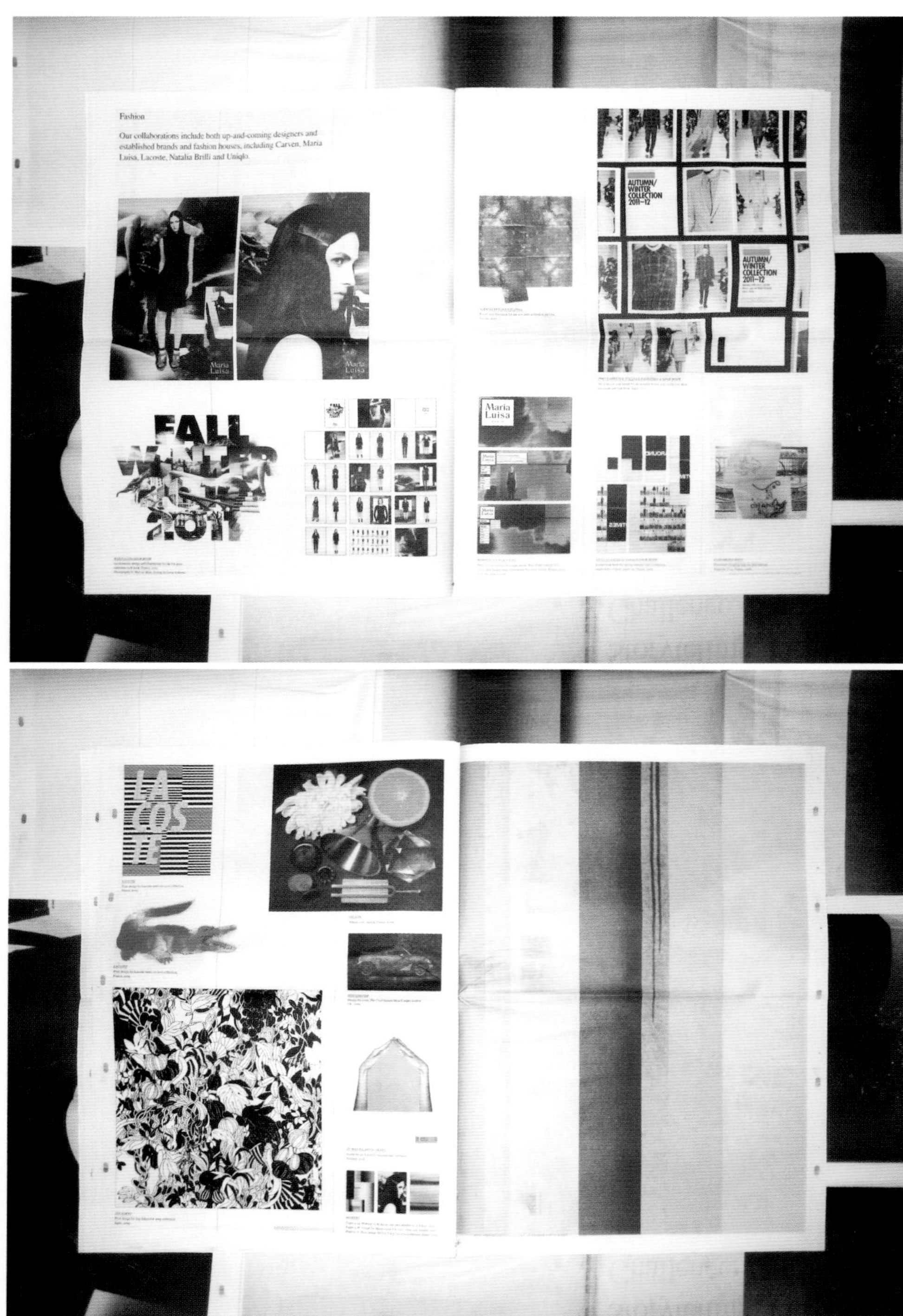
Fashion
Our collaborations include both up-and-coming designers and established brands and fashion houses, including Carven, Maria Luisa, Lacoste, Natalia Brilli and Uniqlo.
Maria Luisa
FALL WINTER 2011
AUTUMN/ WINTER COLLECTION 2011–12
LA COS TE

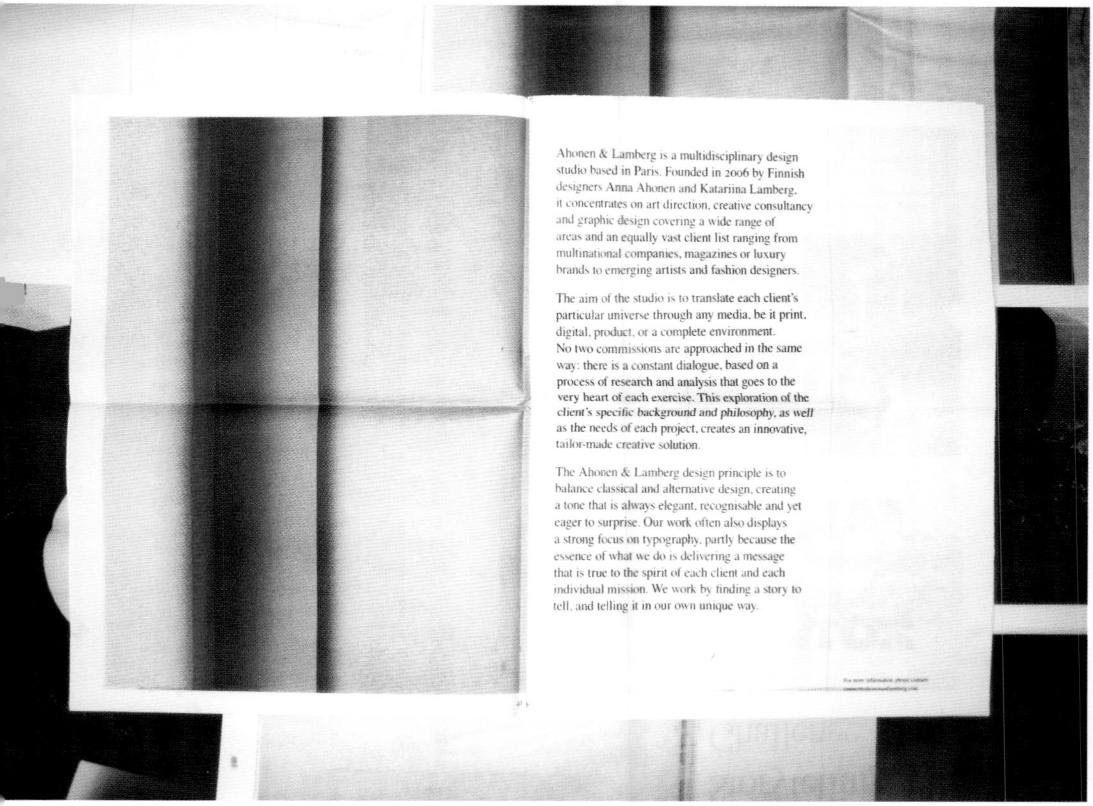

Ahonen & Lamberg is a multidisciplinary design studio based in Paris. Founded in 2006 by Finnish designers Anna Ahonen and Katariina Lamberg, it concentrates on art direction, creative consultancy and graphic design covering a wide range of areas and an equally vast client list ranging from multinational companies, magazines or luxury brands to emerging artists and fashion designers.

The aim of the studio is to translate each client's particular universe through any media, be it print, digital, product, or a complete environment. No two commissions are approached in the same way: there is a constant dialogue, based on a process of research and analysis that goes to the very heart of each exercise. This exploration of the client's specific background and philosophy, as well as the needs of each project, creates an innovative, tailor-made creative solution.

The Ahonen & Lamberg design principle is to balance classical and alternative design, creating a tone that is always elegant, recognisable and yet eager to surprise. Our work often also displays a strong focus on typography, partly because the essence of what we do is delivering a message that is true to the spirit of each client and each individual mission. We work by finding a story to tell, and telling it in our own unique way.

John Lawrence Sullivan
Spring/Summer 2013 Show Invitation
2012 — Invitation
Client John Lawrence Sullivan
Design Ahonen & Lamberg

Show invitation for Paris men's fashion week, design and its use of colors is inspired by the beautiful John Lawrence Sullivan ss 2013 collection.

"Works perfectly with the collection's inspirations"

Ahonen & Lamberg's Favorite Times Letter is "M".

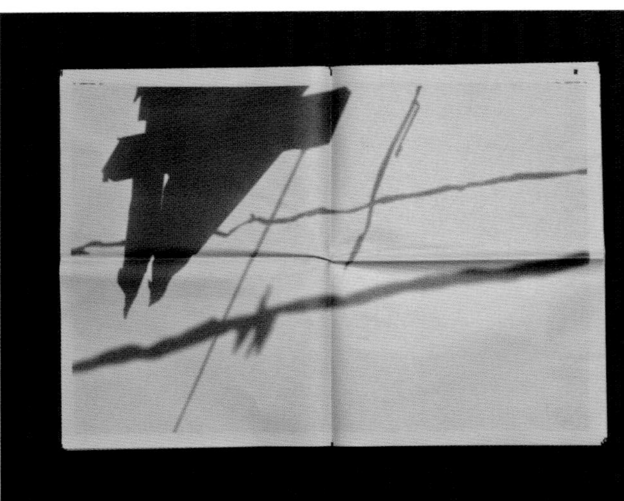

Urbino Times
2009 — Newspaper
Design Catrin Sonnabend

Urbino is a walled city in the Marche region of Italy, southwest of Pesaro. It is a World Heritage Site notable for a remarkable historical legacy of independent Renaissance culture. Staying there for two weeks, I had the impression that through the ages, the architecture of Urbino remained completely unchanged. So I started to look for something moving.

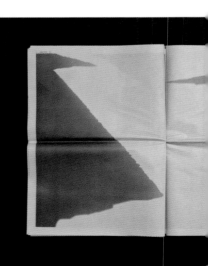

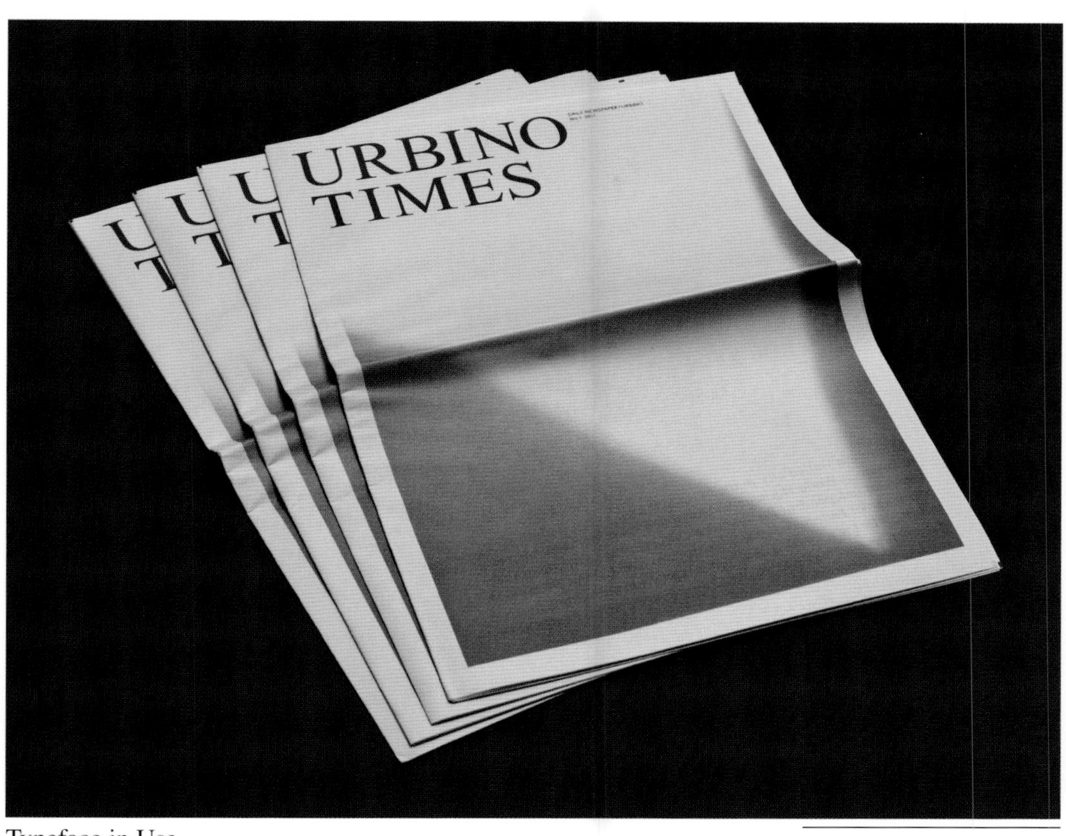

Typeface in Use
Times New Roman,
New Johnston Light

N

"I was looking for a classical Newspaper Font as the Newspaper itself is not a classical one. So it was clear, that it has to be Times."

Catrin Sonnabend's Favorite Times Letter is "N".

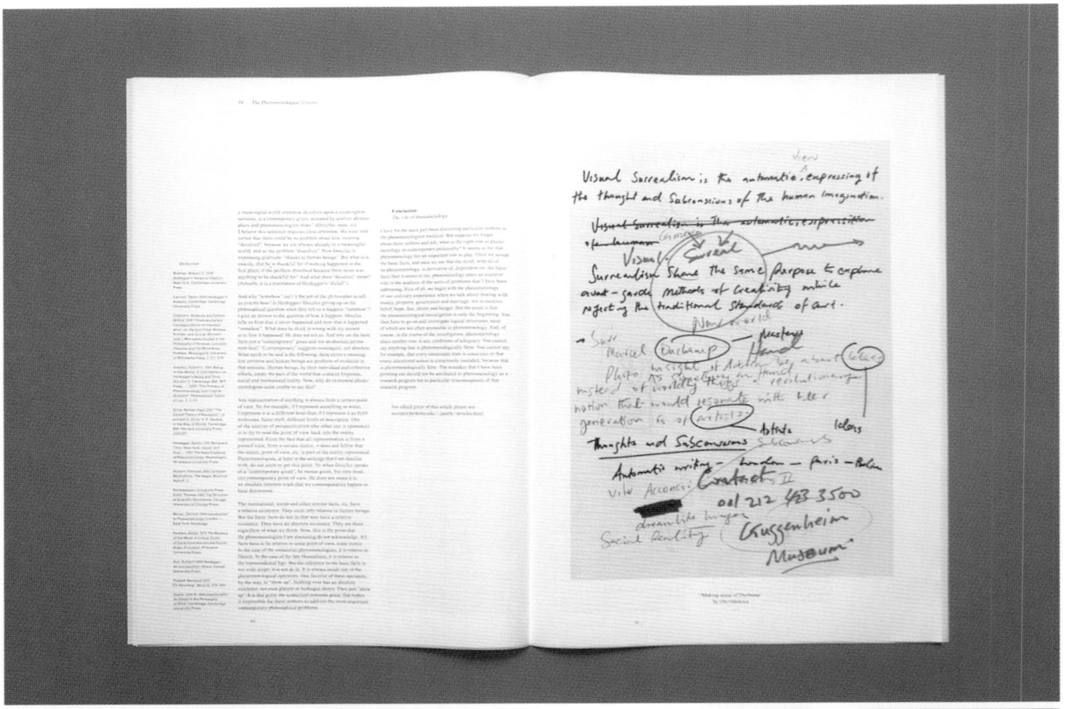
Visual Surrealism is the automatic view expressing of the thought and Subconscious of the human Imagination.
Surrealism Share the same Purpose to explore avant-garde methods of creativity while rejecting the traditional Standards of art.
Marcel Duchamp
Thoughts and Subconscious
Automatic writing — London — Paris — Berlin
001 212 423 3500
Guggenheim Museum.

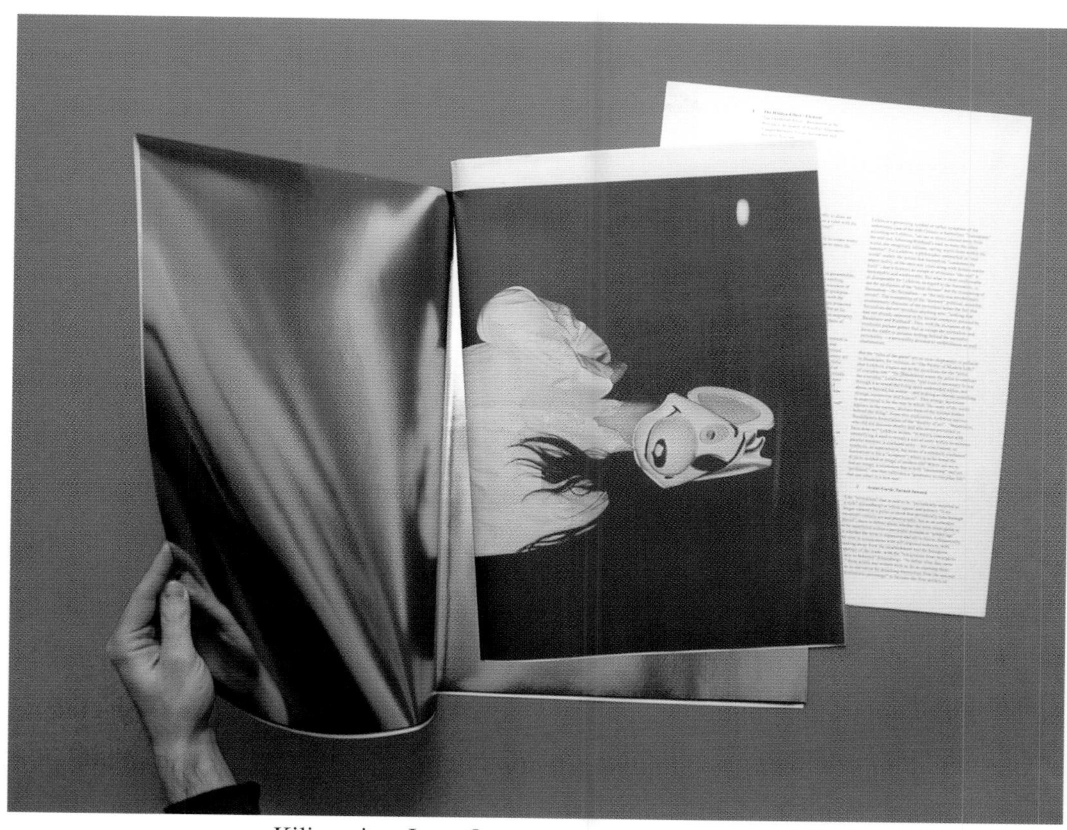

Kilimanjaro Issue 8
2009 — Magazine
Client Kilimanjaro Art & Design, London
Design Gloor & Jandl, Olu Odukoya

Issue 8 of the London based large-sized Kilimanjaro Magazine entitled "The Unofficial Artist". It combines contributions from different art disciplines including fashion, photography, illustration and fine art. The magazine consists of three different sections, a poster and an A4 supplement.

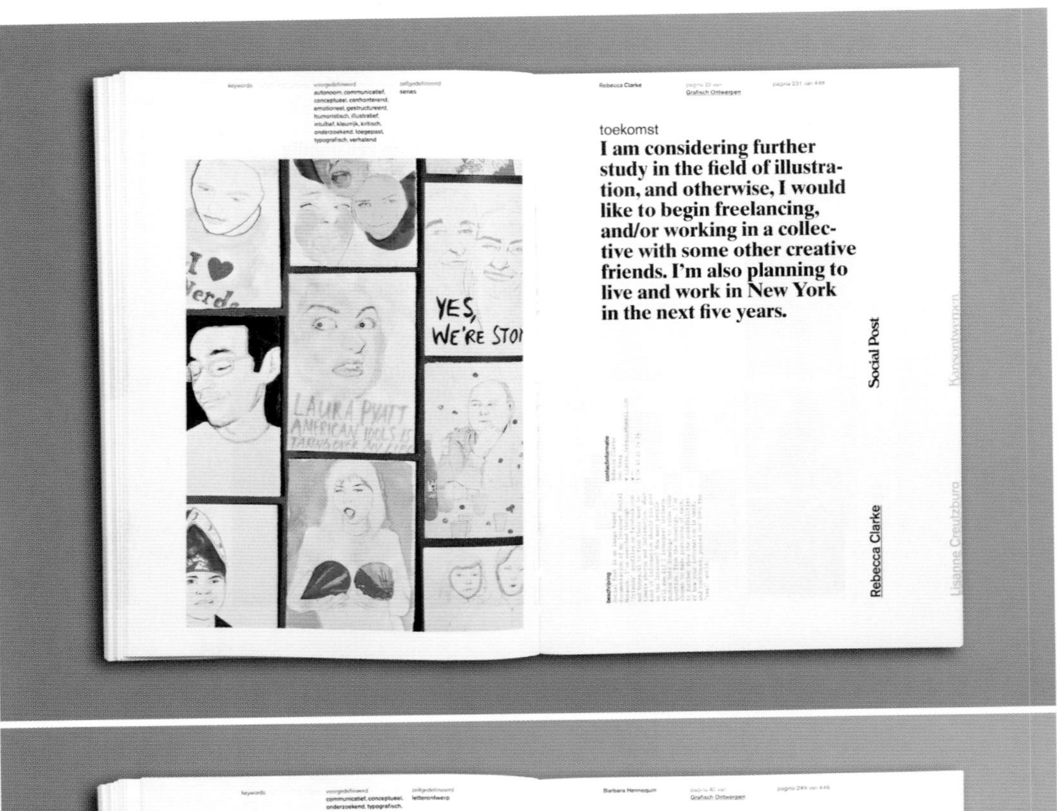

(...)
"All that I have to say has already crossed your mind," said he.
"Then possibly my answer has crossed yours," I replied.
"You stand fast?"
"Absolutely!"
(...)

toekomst
Werken in een klein collectief van ontwerpers van verschillende disciplines, nog meer letters maken, extra veel potloodpunten slijpen, mooie boeken ontwerpen, stomme woordgrapjes maken, obsessief door mijn atlas bladeren, voor me uit staren en dit plan een keer herschrijven.

Overzien

Barbara Hennequin

Typeface in Use
Times Ten

"I like the 'bold formality' of it."

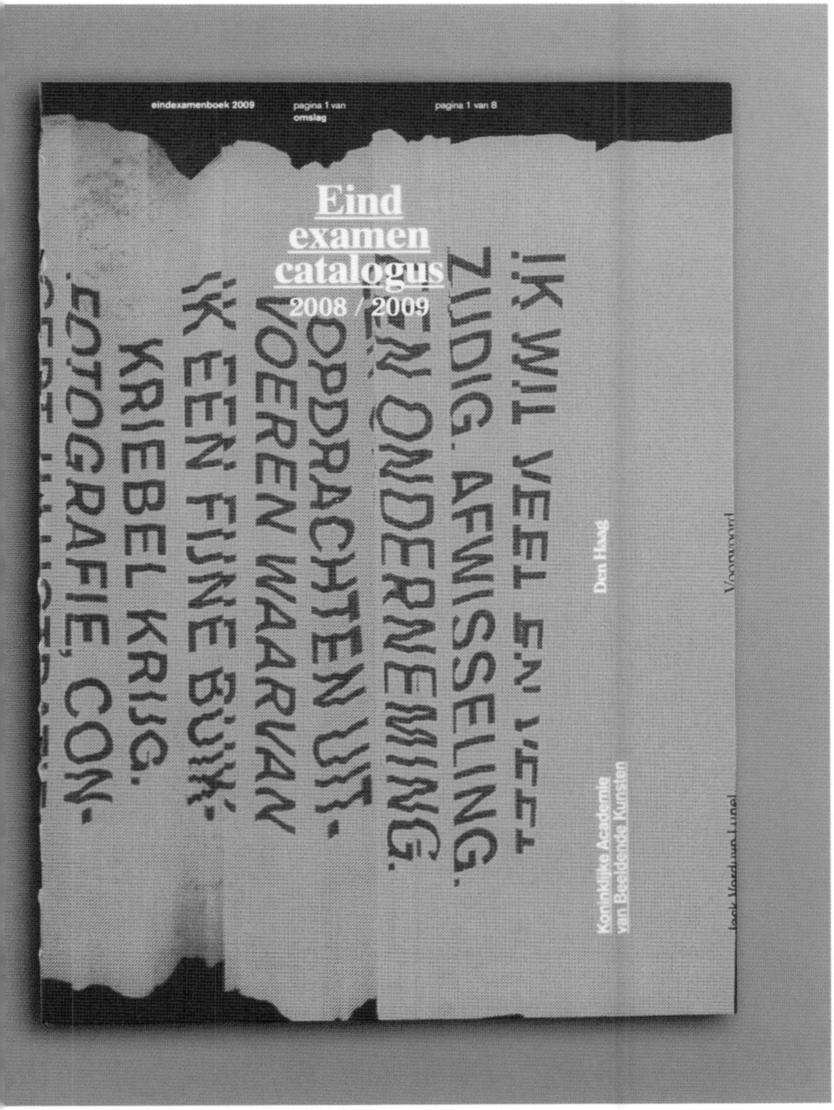

KABK Graduation Catalog 2009
2009 — Book
Client The Royal Academy of Art (KABK), The Hague, the Netherlands.
Design Rob van den Nieuwenhuizen, Mattijs de Wit

Instead of focusing on just the work the students have produced during their graduation period, we asked students about their future plans. Their answers became the main design element — next to the images of their work — in this 452-page book.

The students also had to tag their work with predefined and self-defined keywords, which showed how students of specific courses think of their own work and how this differs among courses.

R

Rob van den Nieuwenhuizen & Mattijs de Wit's Favorite Times Letter is "R".

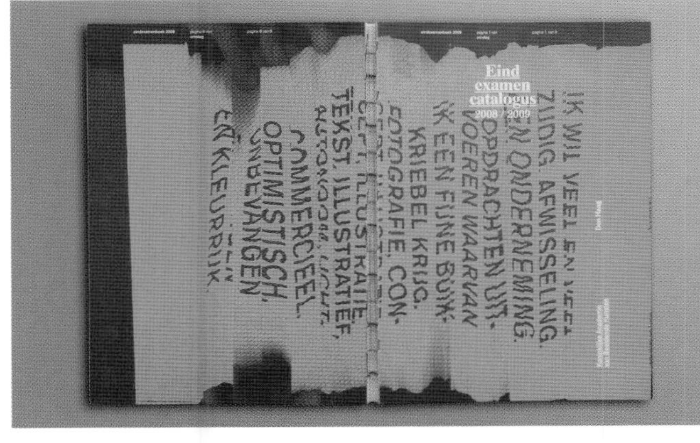

B Sides Festival 17./18.6.11
Sonnenberg Kriens/Luzern
LINE UP
01 The Go! Team
02 DeVotchKa
03 Herman Dune
04 Future of the Left
05 Felix Kubin
06 Attwenger
07 Koudlam
08 Honey For Petzi
09 Paris Suit Yourself
10 Talibam! feat Sam Kulik
11 Grey Mole
12 Must have Been Tokyo
13 Evelinn Trouble & TV Religion
14 GeilerAsDu
15 El Ritschi
16 Dead Bunny
17 Huck Finn
18 Marochine
19 Ophelia's Iron Vest
20 QCID
21 De Haderi
22 Shady and the Vamp
23 Flohzirkus
24 Pirmin Setz und Myrta Amstad
25 MT Dancefloor
26 Ostkost DJ Kollektiv
27 Wicked Wiggler
28 DJ Dizzy Tizzy
29 Kinderprogramm
DANKE
b-sides.ch
WEB

B-Sides Festival
2011 — Poster Series
Client B-Sides Festival
Design Felix Pfäffli

Every time a new band was booked we uploaded its name on the festival's page. On that page anyone could upload the pictures that he thought are representative for an act. Like that we got a pure visual concept of the various artists. The poster shows almost the entire collection. Without order. In addition, the images were printed in the festival's newspaper classified according to the specific act.

B
Sides
Festi–
val
17./
18.6.
11
Sonnen–
berg
Kriens/
Lu–
zern
06
DANKE
12
12
b-sides
.ch
WEB
03
17
21
LINE UP
01 The Go! Team
02 DeVotchKa
03 Herman Dune
04 Future of the Left
05 Felix Kubin
06 Attwenger
07 Koudlam
08 Honey For Petzi
09 Paris Suit Yourself
10 Talibam! feat Sam Kulik
11 Grey Mole
12 Must have Been Tokyo
13 Evelinn Trouble & TV Religion
14 GeilerAsDu
15 El Ritschi
16 Dead Bunny
17 Huck Finn
18 Marochine
19 Ophelia's Iron Vest
20 QCID
21 De Haderi
22 Shady and the Vamp
23 Flohzirkus
24 Pirmin Setz und Myrta Amstad
25 MT Dancefloor
26 Ostkost DJ Kollektiv
27 Wicked Wiggler
28 DJ Dizzy Tizzy
DANKE
20
11
09
08
01
13
DANKE
10
DANKE
05

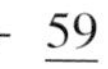

"The festival program was printed on a newspaper. Therefore it was obvious to use Times."

B
Sides
Festi-
val
17./
18.6.
11

LINE UP

01 The Go! Team
02 DeVotchKa
03 Herman Dune
04 Future of the Left
05 Felix Kubin
06 Attwenger
07 Koudlam
08 Honey For Petzi
09 Paris Suit Yourself
10 Talibam! feat Sam Kulik
11 Grey Mole
12 Must have Been Tokyo
13 Evelinn Trouble & TV Religion
14 GeilerAsDu
15 El Ritschi
16 Dead Bunny
17 Huck Finn
18 Marochine
19 Ophelia's Iron Vest
20 QCID

Sonnen-
berg
Kriens/
Lu-
zern

b-sides
.ch
WEB

DANKE

21 De Haderi
22 Shady and the Vamp
23 Flohzirkus
24 Pirmin Setz und Myrta Amstad
25 MT Dancefloor
26 Ostkost DJ Kollektiv
27 Wicked Wiggler
28 DJ Dizzy Tizzy

SCHÜRCH GETRÄNKE ROTHENBURG
DANKE

Martin Parr,
fotografia i col·leccionisme

Exposició al CCCB, fins al 21.10.2012

Souvenir

Martin Parr,
fotografía y coleccionismo

Exposición en el CCCB, hasta el 21.10.2012

Souvenir

Martin Parr,
photography and collecting

Exhibition at the CCCB, until 21.10.2012

Souvenir

Martin Parr,
fotografia i col·leccionisme

Typeface in Use
Times LT Std

Souvenir.
Martin Parr, photography and collecting
2012 — Visual Identity
Client CCCB
Design TwoPoints.Net

This exhibition "Souvenir. Martin Parr, photography and collecting" explores the work of Martin Parr as a prime illustration of the surprising relations between photography and collecting in the context of the touristic experience.

The show examines whether Parr's photography seeks to intervene in reality at an analytical level or whether it consists in recording percussive images that are in general shocking, grotesque or outright kitsch, with a purely illustrative or aesthetic end.

The aim is to link photography and collecting in terms of their shared creative choice-appropriation, an act to which much contemporary artistic thinking has entrusted the creative-artistic phenomenon. The idea is to establish a dialog between two realities (photography and collecting) that reveals their affinities and contradictions, and allows the spectator to decipher the motives, means and objectives of these two forms of artistic intervention.

TwoPoints.Net had to create a visual identity for the exhibition that would be respectful with the work and show both, photography and collected items. The most efficient solution was to use an "invisible" typeface, the subtle gesture of piling up different pictures and a lot of white in the background, which gives the banners and poster a great visibility in the streets.

Souvenir

Martin Parr,
fotografia i col·leccionisme

Exposició al CCCB, fins al 21.10.2012

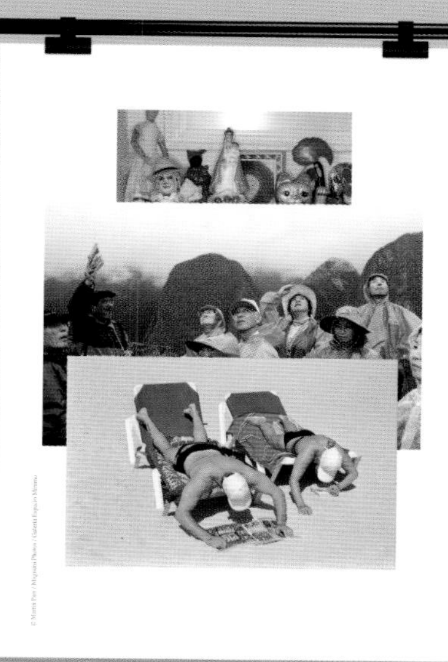

Souvenir

Martin Parr, fotografia i col·leccionisme

Exposició al CCCB, fins al 21.10.2012

Souvenir

Martin Parr, fotografia i col·leccionisme

Exposició al CCCB, fins al 21.10.2012

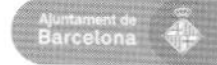

New model management agency TESS Management launched in September, to replace Independent Models – and owners Tori Edwards and Siân Steel couldn't be more excited about the challenge that lies ahead.

"This new venture gives us the opportunity to utilise the experience we have gained over the last two decades and enables us to focus on offering structured personal management to a select number of clients," one half of TESS, Siân Steel, said. The duo, who have decades of fashion industry experience between them, have developed and nurtured some of the industry's most familiar faces; including Erin O'Connor, Georgia Jagger, Karen Elson, Naomi Campbell, Jerry Hall, Thandie Newton, Elizabeth Jagger and Elizabeth Hurley – all of whom they will continue to represent at TESS Management.

"It has become increasingly important for talent to not allow themselves to be pigeon-holed into one sector of the industry," Tori Edwards asserted. "We develop our clients as potential brands that can infiltrate all genres of the media industry be it fashion, TV, music or advertising."

LIZZIE TOVELL

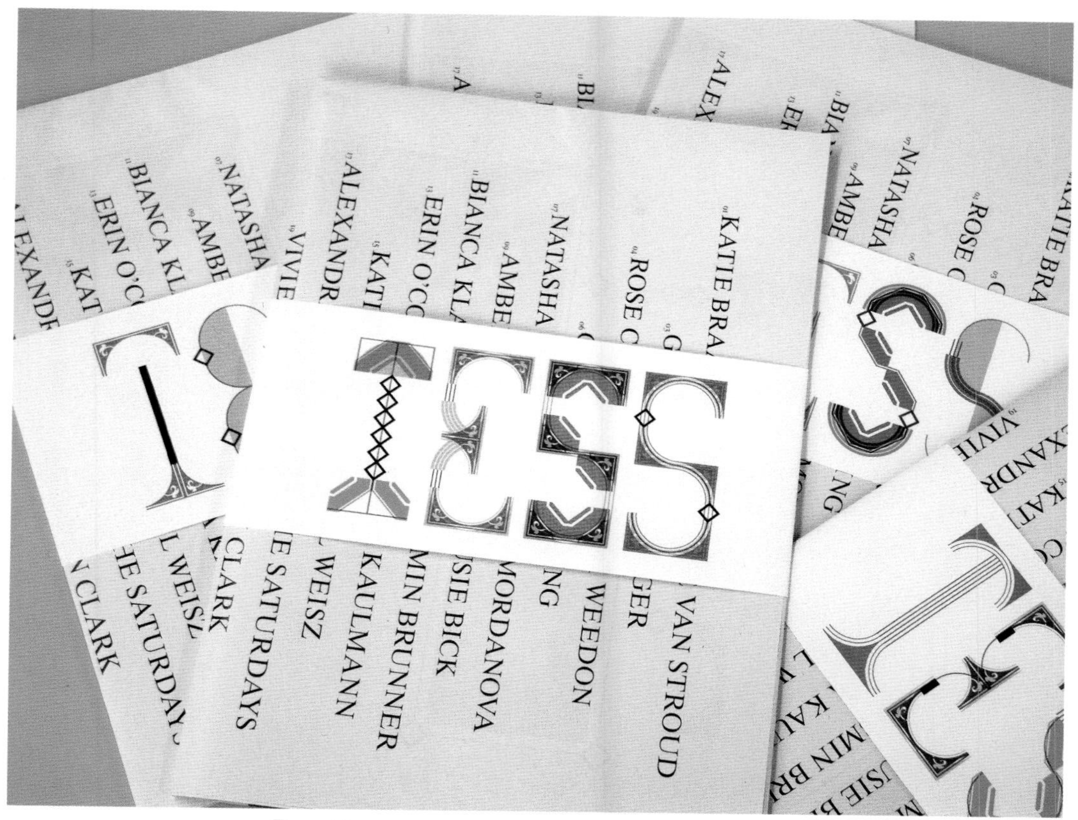

Tess Management
2009 — Visual Identity
Client Tess Management
Creative Direction Mind Design (Holger Jacobs)
Design Mind Design (Sara Streule, Johannes Höhmann), Simon Egli

Identity for a London-based model agency. Tess represents well-established names such as Naomi Campbell and Erin O'Connor in the UK. The identity uses several logo variations based on a modular system of Art Deco inspired elements. The same elements are being used for frames (which overlap images of the models) on various printed applications and on the website.

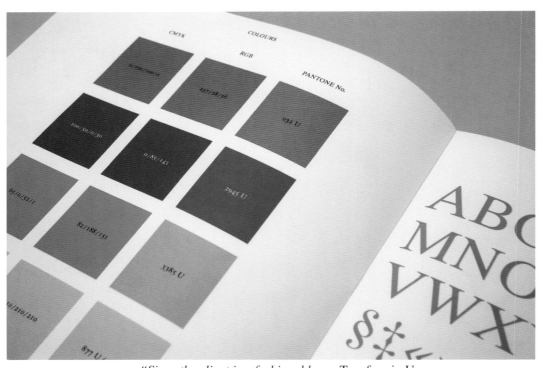

"Since the client is a fashionable model agency we wanted to use a typeface that is in contrast unfashionably common and on everyone's computer."

Typeface in Use
Times Ten LT Std Roman Regular

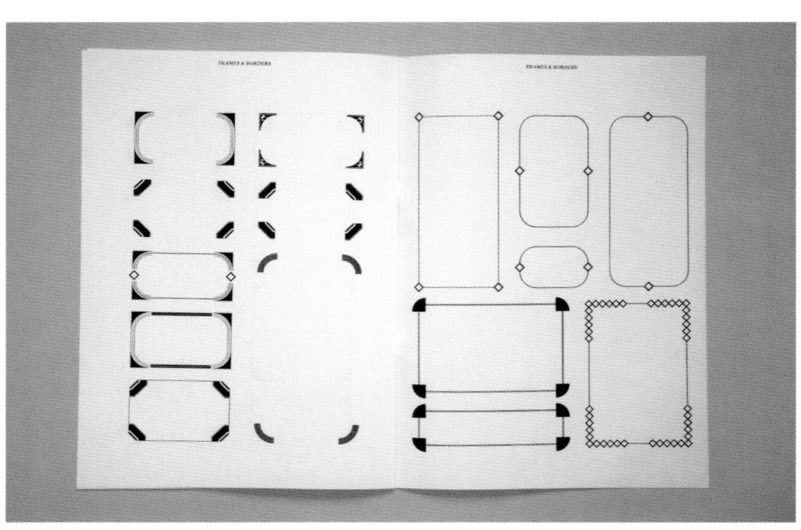

INTRODUCTION

The purpose of this simple design manual is not to establish corporate rules but to illustrate the concept of the TESS logo and its related graphic elements.

Logo Grid

The TESS logo is based on a grid of squares and half-squares. The basic letterforms can be overlaid with a number of additional decorative elements based on the same grid.

TESS Logo & Variations

The number and density of decorative elements allows for a variety of logos ranging from detailed and dense to fragile and light.

Logo Construction

The various logoforms are constructed by using the following three sets: Basic Letterforms, Additional Elements A, Additional Elements B.

Colours

Navy Blue, Red, Turquise Green, Black, Grey and Cream. In print, Black and Grey can be replaced with special finishing techniques such as embossing or die-cutting.

Frames & Borders

Frames are constructed using the same elements as the letterforms. The size of the frame elements should be the same size as in the logo. The shape of a frame can be re-sized vertically as well as horizontally by expanding its connecting lines.

LOGO GRID

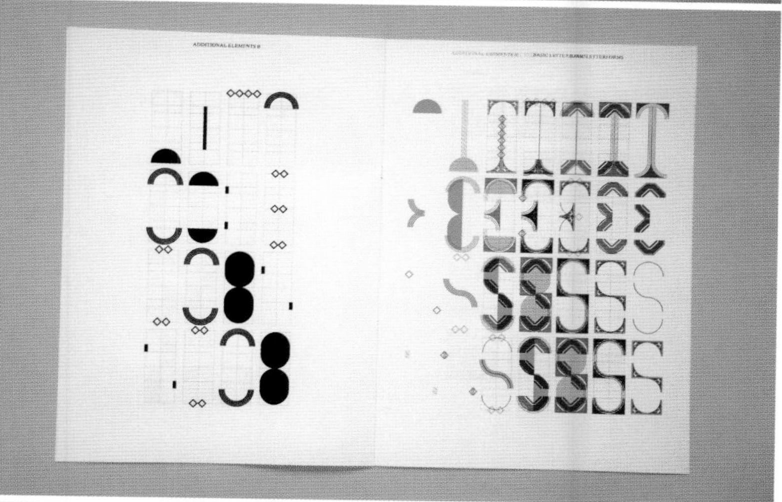

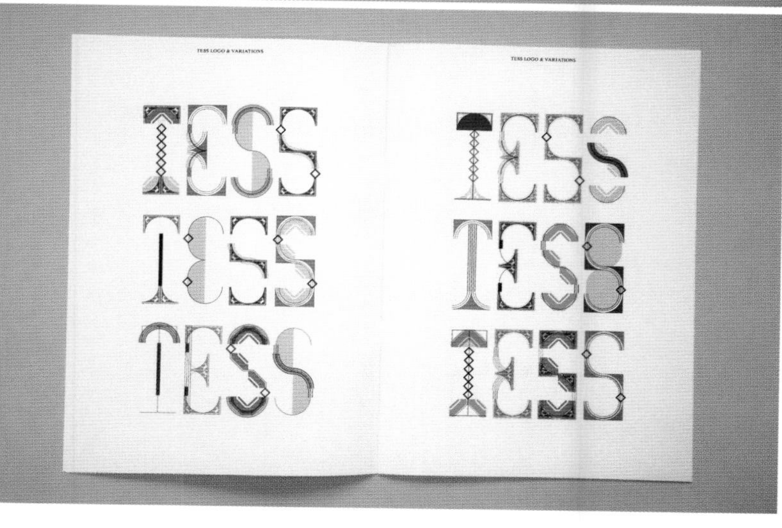

T

Mind Design's Favorite Times Letter is "T".

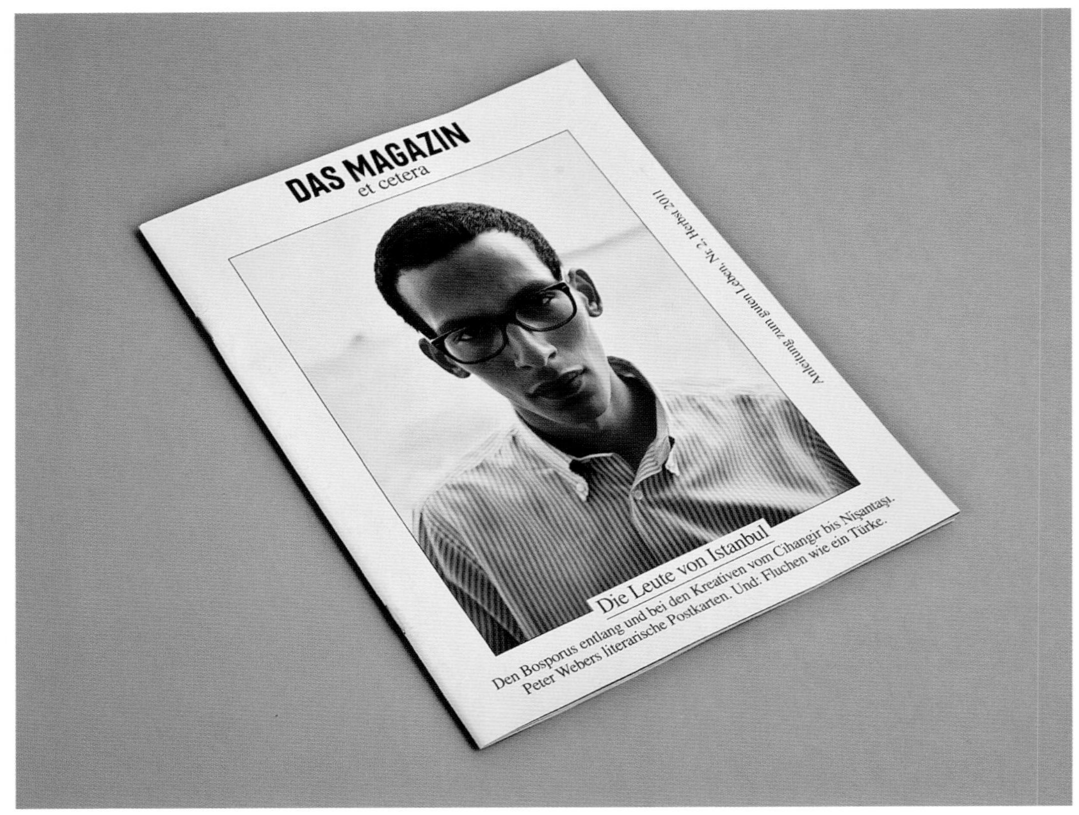

DAS MAGAZIN et cetera
2011 — Magazine
Client Tamedia AG
Design Raffinerie AG für Gestaltung

DAS MAGAZIN et cetera expands the journal DAS MAGAZIN and shows different lifestyles from a journalistic point of view. Every issue spotlights a specific country or city. This issue focused on "The People of Istanbul" and shows the colorful life around the Bosporus.

g

Raffinerie AG für Gestaltung's Favorite Times Letter is "g".

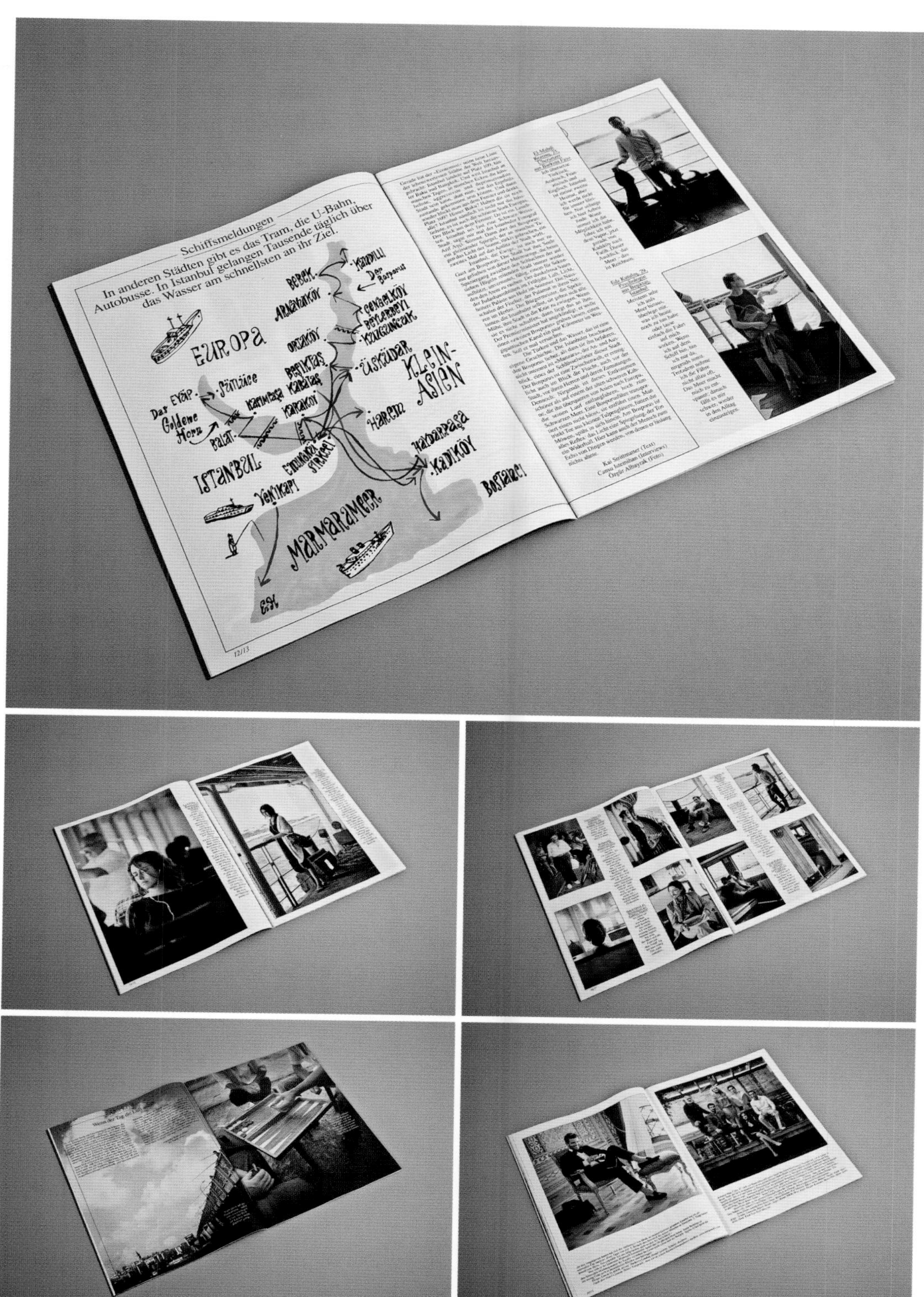
Schiffsmeldungen
In anderen Städten gibt es das Tram, die U-Bahn, Autobusse. In Istanbul gelangen Tausende täglich über das Wasser am schnellsten an ihr Ziel.
EUROPA
KLEIN-ASIEN
ISTANBUL
MARMARAMEER
ÜSKÜDAR
KADIKÖY
BEBEK
ORTAKÖY
KARAKÖY
EMINÖNÜ
SIRKECI
HAYDARPASA
YENIKAPI
BOSTANCI
BALAT
Das Goldene Horn
Der Bosporus
12/13

«Hier in Çukurcuma fühle ich mich geschützt, das Quartier atmet Freiheit aus und stellt sich quer. Dennoch spüre ich, dass es in Istanbul enger wird. Erst recht nach dem letzten grossen Wahlsieg Erdogans. Kürzlich trat ein neues Gesetz in Kraft, danach dürfen Restaurants und Bars keinen Alkohol mehr auf der Strasse ausschenken. In meiner Kunst arbeite ich viel mit Glas. Dabei greife ich oft auf Motive aus dem Osmanischen Reich zurück, was mir immer wieder religiöse Kunden beschert. Dadurch bleibe ich als Freigeist im Kontakt mit den Religiösen, was eigentlich ganz gut ist.

Nahide Büyükkaymakcı, 50, war die erste Frau, die eine Moschee ausstattete. Die Künstlerin hat in Istanbul, Venedig und Berlin studiert. Seit 40 Jahren lebt sie mit Unterbrechungen in Istanbul.

Nahide: Overall: Yohji Yamamoto; Kimono: Erol Albayrak

36/37

«Istanbul ist weder Ost noch West. Okay, vielleicht mehr West, aber trotzdem eigenständig. Was ich eigentlich sagen will: Ich bin kein türkischer Mann, ich bin ein Mann aus Istanbul.»

Für den 41-jährigen Modedesigner Ümit Ünal ist sein Nachname – «Ünal» steht im Türkischen für «Werde berühmt!» – längst Wirklichkeit. Ünal (hier mit seiner Muse, dem Model Didem Soydan) ist das Aushängeschild der türkischen Modeindustrie und hat dabei so ziemlich alle Modepreise abgeräumt, welche die Türkei zu vergeben hat. Seine Kleider sind Kunst und Mode in einem und wurden auf allen grossen internationalen Laufstegen präsentiert.

Alle Kleider: Ümit Ünal

FENERB
FEN

1
Kleiner Teppich von Carpet
2
Krawatte von ZARA
3
4
5
Fan-Schal, privat

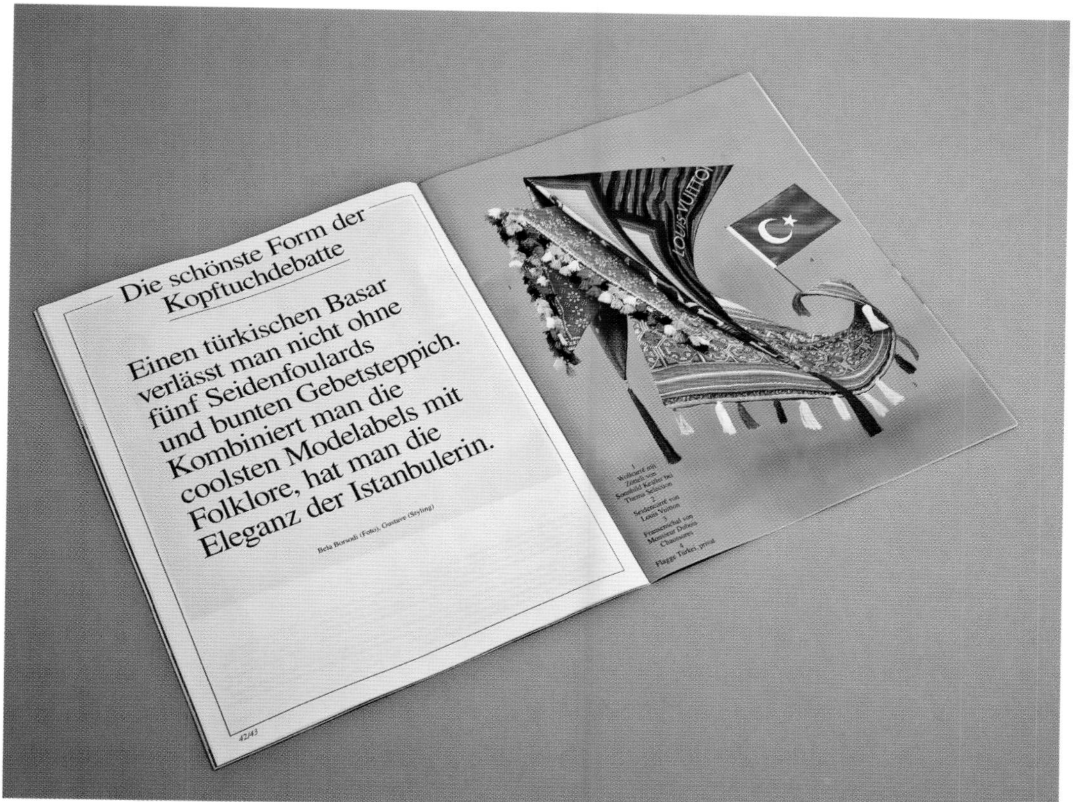

Die schönste Form der Kopftuchdebatte

Einen türkischen Basar verlässt man nicht ohne fünf Seidenfoulards und bunten Gebetsteppich. Kombiniert man die coolsten Modelabels mit Folklore, hat man die Eleganz der Istanbulerin.

Bela Borsodi (Foto), Gustave (Styling)

1
Wollcarré mit
Zottelei von
Sonnhild Kestler bei
Thema Selection
2
Seidencarré von
Louis Vuitton
3
Fransenschal von
Monsieur Dubois
Chaussures
4
Flagge Türkei, privat

Danish Fashion Institute
Annual Report
Client Danish Fashion Institute
Design Homework

Annual Report for the Danish Fashion Institute, an organization which promotes fashion, created by and for the Danish fashion industry.

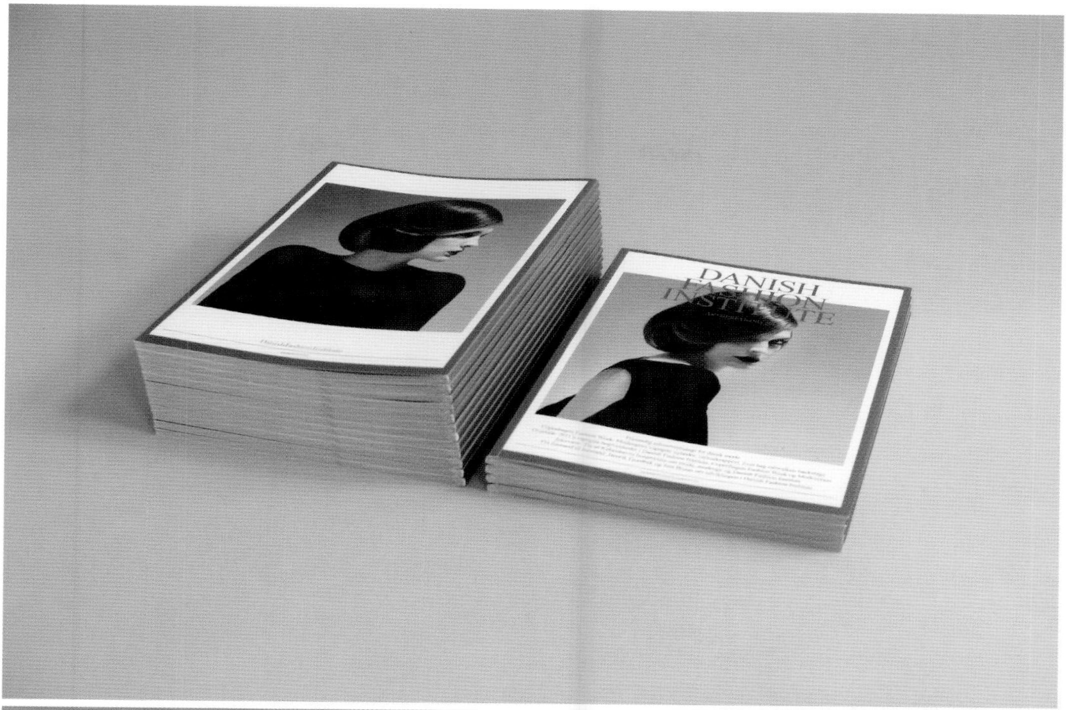
DANISH
FASHION
INSTITUTE

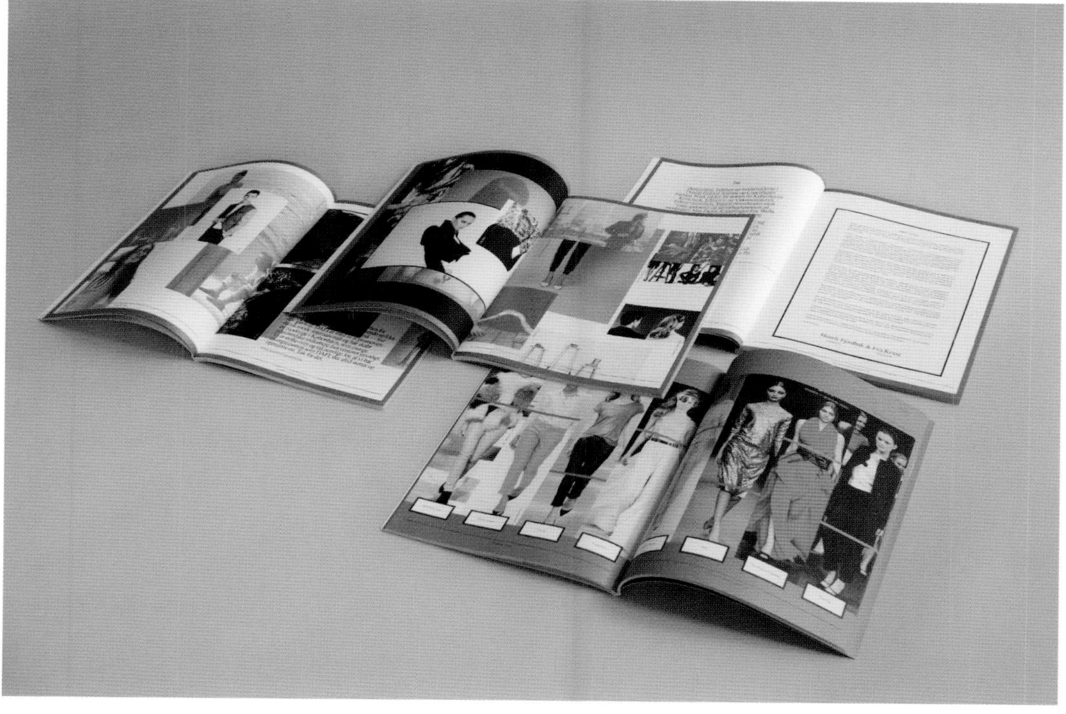

FLYING A
WOMEN'S AND MEN'S
CLOTHING

RE-ESTABLISHED 2012
FLYING A
WOMEN'S AND MEN'S
CLOTHING

RE-ESTABLISHED 2012
FLYING A
WOMEN'S AND MEN'S
CLOTHING

Flying A
2012 — Visual Identity
Client Flying A Agency
Design Homework

"Flying A" is a progressive sales agency in the fashion industry offering a carefully selected brand portfolio for the quality-aware retailer. Creating a united front with their clients, "Flying A Agency" always aspires to deliver the best market service through a sincere brand and customer dedication, where communication is key.

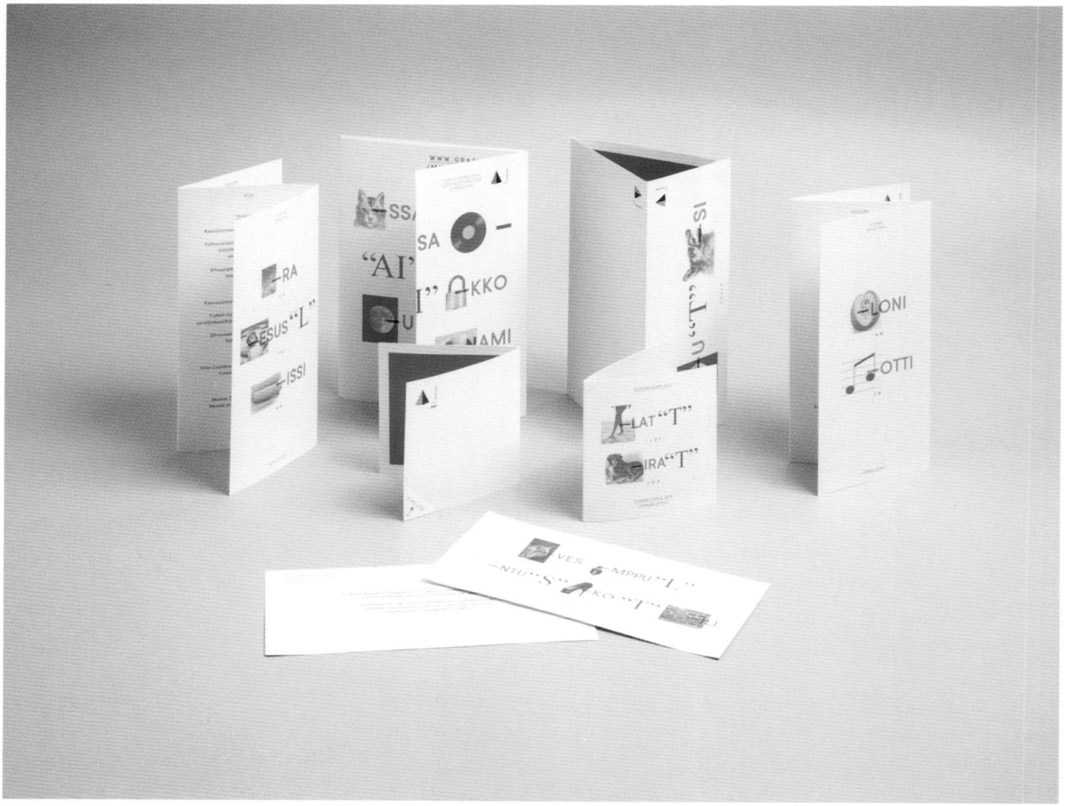

Typeface in Use
Times New Roman Regular, Sofia, Sofia Bold

"Sofia because it looks good and is neutral in a proper way. Times because it's the most default font you can imagine."

Vuoden Huiput 2010
2010 — Visual Identity, Invitation, Brochure, Yearbook, Web Application
Client Grafia ry
Design Tsto

With Vuoden Huiput (The Best of the Year in Finnish advertising and design) we wanted to experiment with the relatively dubious and unpredictable nature of crowdsourcing and the visual language of anonymous internet users. Together with a programer we created an application that transformed any written word or sentence into a rebus, an allusional device that uses pictures to represent words or parts of words. In English, a rebus often uses homonyms, as seen in the classic IBM logo consisting of a picture of an eye, a picture of a bee and the letter M. However, homonyms are rare in Finnish language, therefore a rebus was constructed from a list of some 5000 words with the most used syllables and matched with an image search result from Google.

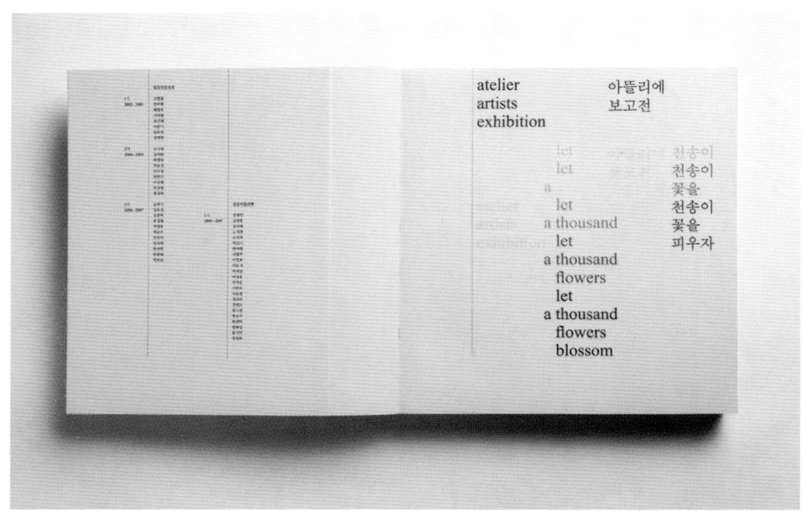

workroom's Favorite Times Ligature is “fi”.

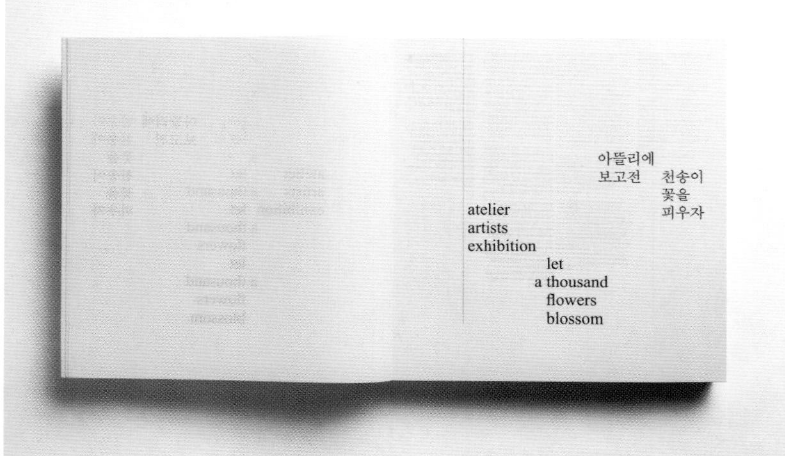

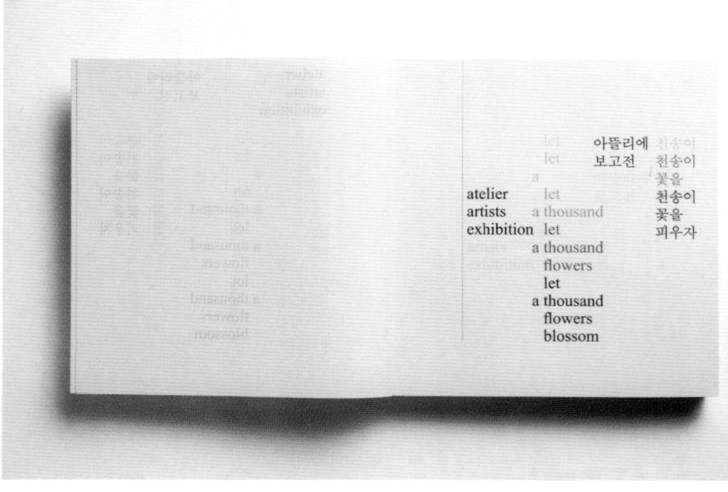

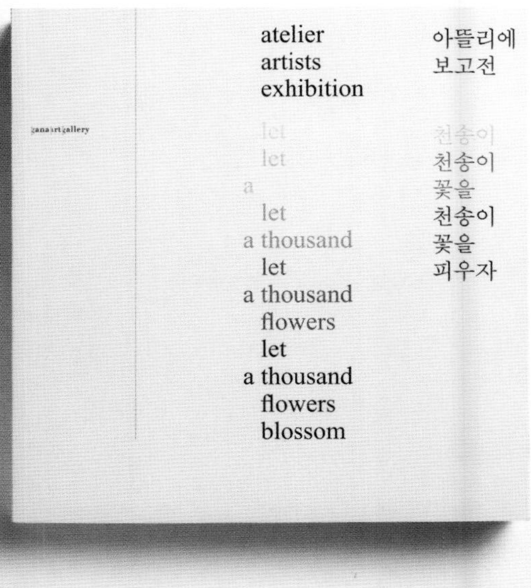

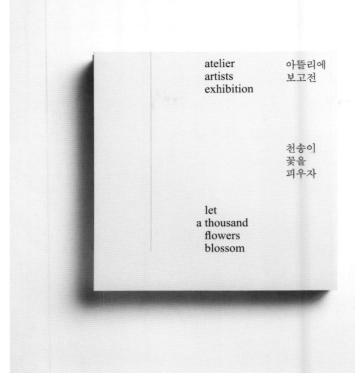

Let a thousand flowers blossom
2008 — Book Design
Client Gana Art Gallery
Design workroom

"Let a thousand flowers blossom" is an exhibition book in the form of a report on 34 residency artists of Gana Art Center Atelier. The title was after Mao Zedong's political slogan "a hundred flowers bloom, a hundred schools of thought contend." Just as the title indicates, diverse works of art were printed in the exhibition book. Figuratively, artists like Jenson, Lublain Graph, and American Typewriter were contending with one another in a book. At such a time a designer's choice is simple: choosing either a typeface that resembles each artist's voice or one that looks objective like Times New Roman. I picked the latter, and as a result we got a book that is not hated by any artist.

thisislove studio's Favorite Times Letter is "T".

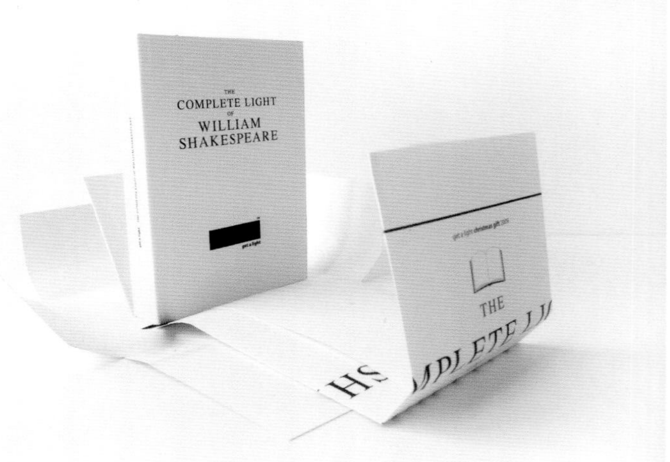

Typeface in Use
Times New Roman

Shakespeare Notebook
2009 — Festive Gift, Notebook, Flyer
Client get a light™
Art Direction/Design thisislove studio (Joana Areal)
Photography thisislove studio, Adriana Pacheco

Christmas gift made especially for "get a light". It is a personal notebook. Each page has a sentence spoken by a character from William Shakespeare, containing the word "light".

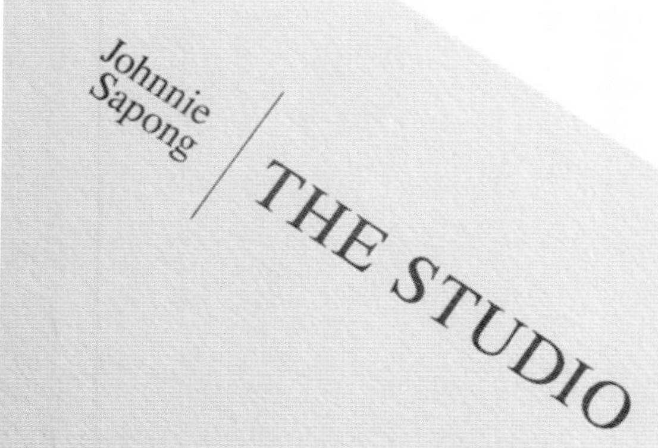

The internationally renowned hair stylist Johnnie Sapong came to Birch when planning to open his first permanent studio. After years of working internationally for the majority of his time Johnnie decided that he needed a base for him and his team in London. The Studio is as much an art gallery for conceptual experimentation as a hair salon. Birch developed a visual identity for The Studio including the logo and stationery. Using detailed typography, the identity works seamlessly against the ever changing background of The Studio as it is redecorated periodically.

Typeface in Use
Times

The Studio
2012 — Visual Identity
Client Johnnie Sapong
Design Birch

Rehearsal
Research
Paul Kajander
Justine Chambers
Holly Ward

Rehearsal Research

Rehearsal Research 4 Sarah Todd

Notes on a Residency

The *Rehearsal Research* residency project was conceived while I was working as a research assistant for the *Vancouver Art in the Sixties* website. Working with photographer Michael de Courcy, I was cataloguing his extensive collection of photographic documentation of Intermedia, Canada's first artist run centre, established in Vancouver in 1967. As I sorted through over 2500 photos, I was struck by the many images of dance and dancers. It became clear that dancers and choreographers played an important role in the development of both artist-run culture and the performative art practices of the 1960s and 1970s—an engagement I had not been wholly aware of.

Modern dance was an important force in establishing Intermedia and artist-run initiatives in Vancouver, which can be traced to one pioneering influence, dancer and choreographer Helen Goodwin. Helen Goodwin was a British born choreographer, trained in the Laban modern dance method, who had worked at UBC in the Physical Education department since 1955. Goodwin was closely involved in organizing the generative Festival of Contemporary Art, which ran from 1963 to 1969, featuring performances by international luminaries Merce Cunningham, Robert Rauschenberg and local agents Iain Baxter and Glenn Lewis. Goodwin was one of the founding members of the Intermedia Society; a collection of visual artists, poets, musicians, filmmakers and dancers that worked out of a number of spaces and exhibited widely between 1967 and 1969.

Rehearsal Research 6 Sarah Todd

At this time, Goodwin directed TheCo. which could be thought of as Intermedia's resident dance company. This was a guiding force within the constellation of activity that was Intermedia. It required regular rehearsals and a great deal of space, demanding Intermedia's large studio on Beatty Street. Helen Goodwin's influence through TheCo. contributed to Intermedia's unprecedented interdisciplinarity and provided a focus on the performative, before "performance art" was a widely used term.

TheCo. was comprised of professional and amateur dancers, including some of Goodwin's UBC Physical Education students. This primarily female dance company performed wherever the Intermedia Society was exhibiting, at the Vancouver Art Gallery, amongst sculptures and early media art installations, and alongside early performance works by Gathie Falk and Glenn Lewis. The images of performance were not the most compelling photographic documentation I encountered. Rather, the images of rehearsal attracted me, as they were more numerous, and because they lacked a certain kind of self-consciousness that comes with costumes and lighting. In many of these images Helen Goodwin stands at a distance, directing, pointing and speaking to the group. She is scrutinizing, squatting, standing, looking. The studio frames these photos: the wide-open warehouse space on Beatty Street with the wooden floors of a dance studio.

The importance of rehearsal and pedagogy in the early days of live performance is perhaps most striking in a 1968 workshop conducted by dancer and choreographer Deborah Hay at the Douglas Gallery in Vancouver. In the few photos that exist from the event, one can observe notable Canadian artists Glenn Lewis, Gathie Falk, Michael Morris, Vincent Trasov and Jorge Zontal, in relaxed positions, standing in the gallery space. This workshop led to subsequent workshops with New York based dancers Yvonne Rainer, Steve Paxton, and Barbara Lloyd. At this time there was, according to Helen Goodwin, "a lot of to and fro between Vancouver and New York."[1] It could also be said there was a second exchange happening, between modern dance practice and visual art production, not just internationally, but also locally in Vancouver. Art historian Clive Robertson connects the genesis of Canadian performance art to Vancouver's relationship with this community of American dancers, specifically the 1968 Douglas Gallery workshop with Deborah Hay.[2]

This important historical connection between modern dance and avant-garde art practice, lead me to question how this relationship could function in the current contemporary art making climate. Where was the

Rehearsal Research 8 Sarah Todd

Rehearsal Research
2011 — Poster, Booklet
Client Western Front
Design Post Projects

This poster was produced to announce the closing reception of "Rehearsal Research" a multidisciplinary residency curated by Sarah Todd. The accompanying program booklet featured an essay by Sarah that described the origins of the residency, and introduced its participants: Justine Chambers, Paul Kajander, and Holly Ward.

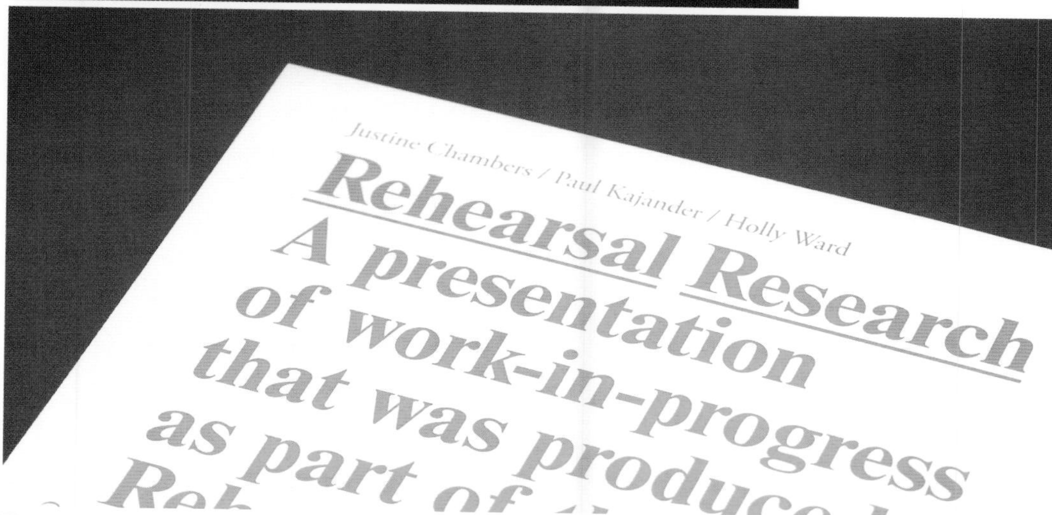

Typeface in Use
Times New Roman MT Bold

"Around the time this project came up, we'd been hearing people make proclamations like 'don't use Times unless you really have to' without much explanation. We didn't agree, and took the next available opportunity to use the typeface."

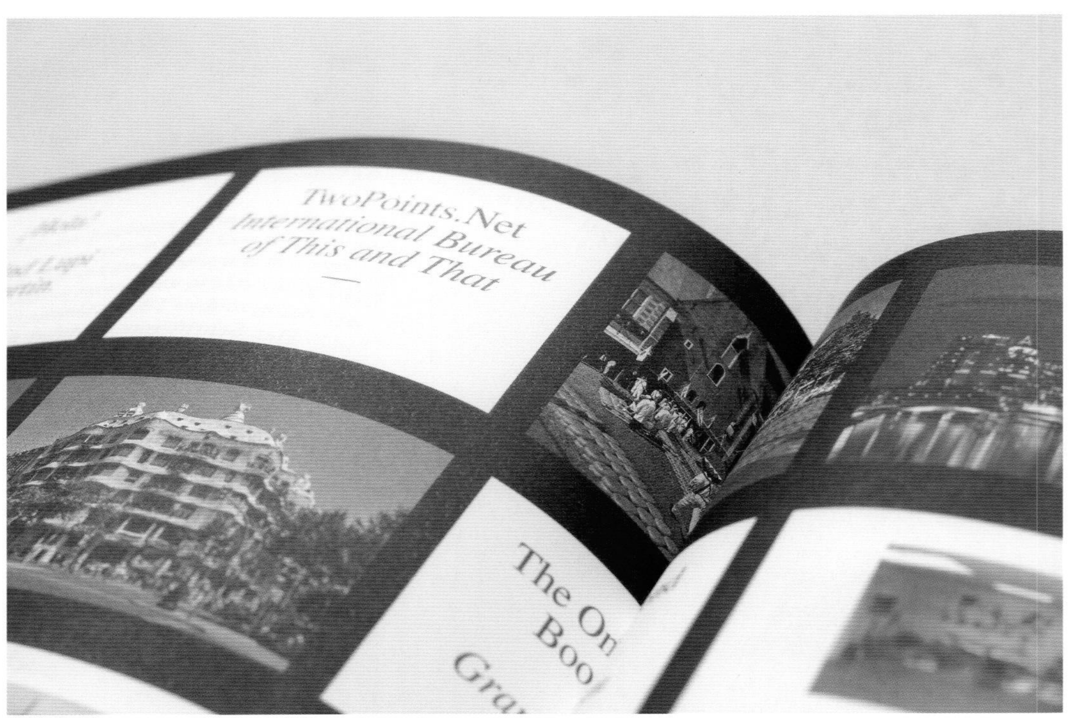

Das Symposium ›Dialog der Schrift: Autorschaft in der Gestaltung‹ fand am 8. und 9. Juli 2011 in Kiel statt. In der Gegenüberstellung heterogener, zeitgenössischer Positionen aus Theorie und Praxis wurde verschiedenen Fragen zur Autorschaft in der Gestaltung nachgegangen.

www.dialogderschrift.de

ISBN 978-3-943763-00-3
Raum für Publikation, 2012

Dialog der Schrift: Autorschaft in der Gestaltung
2012 — Book Design
Client Muthesius Academy of Fine Arts and Design, Kiel
Design Omar Nicolas, Maret Tholen, Hagen Verleger
Photography Slanted Magazin & Weblog, 2012

This publication is a reader for a symposium about authorship in contemporary graphic and book design. It featured both the lecturers' talks as well as an additional part with photos and a bibliography on authorship.

Typeface in Use
Times New Roman MT

"It's a classic baroque serif typeface (with real small caps and old-style figures) which beautifully (and kind of tongue-in-cheek) lean towards the topic of 'authorship in design'."

a

Omar Nicolas, Maret Tholen & Hagen Verleger's Favorite Times Letter is "a".

und Einschübe auf. Die Breite der Texteinschübe ändert sich fortlaufend. Vereinzelt wird der Blocksatz so dünn, dass im Text zwischen den Wörtern ungewöhnliche Zwischenräume entstehen, die man entweder als ›schlecht gesetzt‹ oder eben als bewusste typografische Störungen interpretieren kann. Wiederholt verlässt der Blocksatz seine strenge Gestalt und geht an diesen Stellen in eine mittelachsige oder treppenartige Satzanordnung über.

Der Text will bei Derrida in seiner Schichtung und in seinem Zusammenwirken mit anderen Textelemente verstanden werden. Er kann dadurch ständig neu als auch unterschiedlich interpretiert werden. Die Interpretation setzt sich fort, indem sie das Verdeckte und Unsichtbare des Textes sichtbar macht.

Wie bei Barthes hat auch bei Derrida der Text ein eigenes, vom Autor unabhängiges Verständnis. In seinem Essay *Signatur Ereignis Kontext*[9] stellt Derrida heraus, warum nach dieser Theorie Kontext und Sinn eines Textes nie absolut bestimmbar sind. Danach muss jedes sprachliche oder schriftliche Element »iterierbar«, also wiederholbar und zitierbar sein. Als Spur, die nicht abwesend oder präsent und alleinig im Text bleibendes Sinnmerkmal ist, kann die Schrift trotz der Abwesenheit des Senders oder des Empfängers Sinn herstellen, indem sie immer in einer Vielzahl von Kontexten von verschiedenen Personen gelesen werden kann. Der Text kann außerhalb seiner ursprünglichen Kontexte funktionieren und lässt sich in andere, neue Kontexte einschreiben – ihm aufpfropfen.

Dieser Gedankengang ermöglicht uns einen Bezug zur Typographie herzustellen: Eine typografische Inszenierung kann, indem sie einem vorgegebenen Text eine neue Form verleiht und ihn in einen neuen Kontext stellt und damit weitere Zugangsformen schafft, den Text anders zu verstehen geben.

Das ›zitathafte Aufpfropfen‹ ist nicht nur eine neu eröffnete Möglichkeit des Funktionierens der Schrift, sondern, so Derrida, gehört zur Struktur jedes gespro-

36

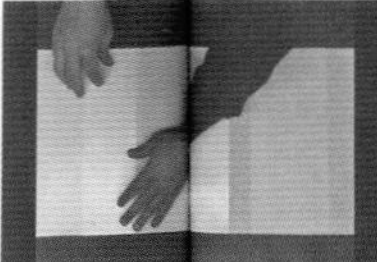

IV

chenen oder geschriebenen Zeichens. Das Herausnehmen eines Zeichens aus seinem Gewebe und das Einschreiben in ein Neues ist somit die Voraussetzung des Funktionierens eines jeden Zeichens.

Dieses Prinzip gilt auch bei der Übersetzung: Wenn die Sprache als differentielles Gewebe gedacht werden kann, kann die Übersetzung von einer Sprache in eine andere nicht einfach einzelne Elemente übertragen, sondern muss immer Verwebungen, Relationen, Verhältnisse und Kontexte mitdenken. Es ist davon auszugehen, dass der Prozess der Übersetzung als sprachlicher Vollzug die Modifikation des sprachlichen Gewebes vorantreibt.

Bei Derrida wechselt die Autorität des Autors ihre Stellung in die der Schrift; der Autor wird zum Medium der Schrift. Als Medium bezeichnet man Figuren, die Inhalte zwischen unterschiedlichen Sphären vermitteln. Der Vermittler wird dabei selbst zum Schöpfer. Als solchen kann man auch die Autorschaft in der Typografie und der Übersetzung verstehen: Wenn der Typograf den Faden der Schrift aufnimmt, ihn webt (lat. *textere*) und auf andere Weise bezeichnen lässt (frz. *désigné*), gibt er ihn weiter und setzt Autorschaft fort.

Die inszenierende Typografie übersetzt demnach die im Text enthaltenen Gedanken in Struktur und Form und stellt so dem Textinhalt eine Interpretation gegenüber. Macht es uns nicht diese prinzipielle Verwandtschaft zwischen der Typografie und der Übersetzung möglich, die Beziehung zwischen beiden als Analogie zu betrachten? Und stellen dabei nicht beide etwas ›Zweites‹ einem ›Ersterem‹ gegenüber? Hier ist nochmals zu betonen, dass die literarische Übersetzung zwar das Original wiedergibt, sie durch die Unterschiede in den Sprachen aber eigene inhaltliche Positionen markieren muss und damit auch einen neuen Text produziert. Ebenso verhält sich für uns die inszenierende Typografie: Sie gibt zwar auch den vorangegangenen Textinhalt wieder, erschafft aber durch ihre Gestaltungsprinzipien und -haltungen eine neue Sprache.

37

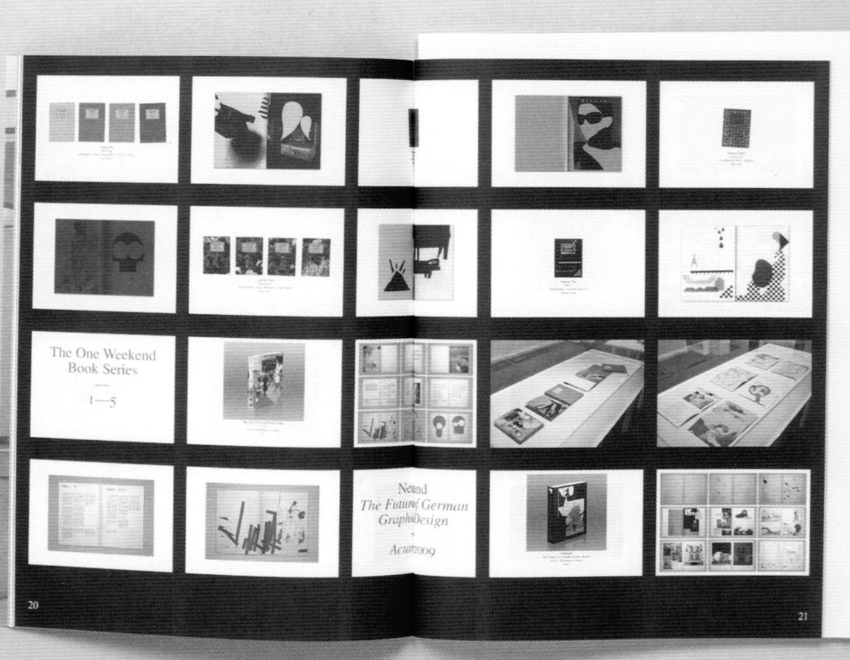

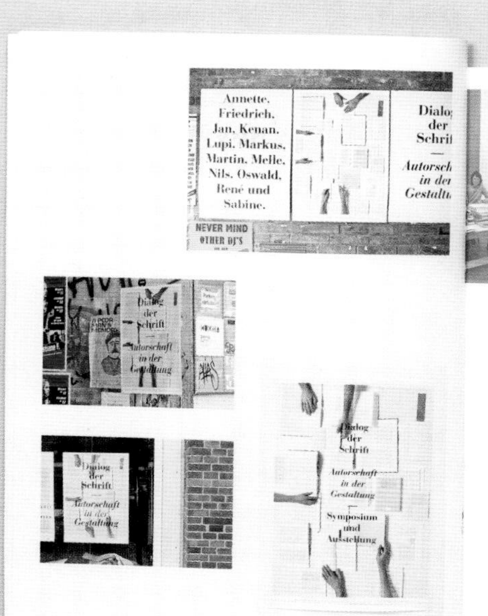

Ich glaube, darin liegt die politische Diskussion dessen, was uns hier beschäftigt. Wie wollen wir produzieren? In welcher Weise können wir gemeinsam produzieren, wie sind die Produzenten im fertigen Produkt letztlich repräsentiert? – Wenn Foucault in seiner Analyse der Autor-Funktion darauf hinweist, dass der Autorenname nicht wie der Eigenname vom Inneren eines Diskurses zum realen, äußeren Individuum geht, das ihn hervorgebracht hat, sondern dass er in gewisser Weise an der Grenze der Texte entlang läuft und dass die Autor-Funktion charakteristisch für die Existenz-, Zirkulations- und Funktionsweise bestimmter Diskurse innerhalb einer Gesellschaft ist, dann wird vielleicht deutlich, dass die polyphone Autorschaft auch eine Form ihrer Repräsentation finden muss.

Meist geschieht das nur im Impressum, während auf dem Titel in der alten Warhol-Manier alle Mitarbeiter unter dem Label des Meisters verschwinden. Oder die Autorschaft wird in unterschiedlichen Kontexten unterschiedlich akzentuiert: An der einen Stelle wird das Buch als eine Leistung des Künstlers wahrgenommen, an anderer Stelle als Leistung des Grafik-Designers, seltener als eine gemeinsame Leistung. Aber vielleicht liegt genau an dieser Stelle auch die Begriffsarbeit, die wir alle gemeinsam noch zu leisten haben: an neuen Formen und Darstellungskonventionen zu arbeiten, um eine kollektive Autorschaft, Ensemble-Arbeit, auch sichtbar zu machen.

Erst dann werden wir nicht mehr darüber stolpern, wenn es heißt »l'autore siamo noi!«.

47

„... ein Gedanke muß plump sein, um im Handeln zu seinem Recht zu kommen." (Walter Benjamin, in: Rezension zu Brechts Dreigroschenroman)

„Uebrigens ist mir Alles verhasst, was mich bloss belehrt, ohne meine Thätigkeit zu vermehren, oder unmittelbar zu beleben." (Goethe, Brief an Schiller, 1791, zitiert nach: Friedrich Nietzsche,: Vom Nutzen und Nachtheil der Historie für das Leben)

„Allgemeine Ansichten zur Literatur habe ich nie gehabt und nie verstanden. Mehr Engagement! Mehr Realismus! Mehr Relevanz! Ist doch alles Quatsch. Sobald Schriftsteller irgendeine Form von Theorie ausmünzen, läuft sie immer sofort darauf hinaus, dass zum allgemeinen Ziel erklärt wird, was der Autor selbst am besten kann und schon seit Jahren praktiziert. Das sind keine Theorien, das ist das, was sich heranbildet in kleinen Hasen, wenn es nachts dunkel wird im großen Wald." (Wolfgang Herrndorfer, Interview in der FAZ, 31. Januar 2011)

»Blickt man auf Rußland, so ändert sich in fünf Jahren alles, aber in 200 Jahren nichts.«

62

Ich finde, daß der Begriff »Autorschaft« für uns Designer heikel ist, weil er arg hoch greift. Er wird vor allem von Literaturwissenschaftlern diskutiert, und zwar auf einem Niveau, das ich als praktischer Designer – und andere gibt es ja nicht – zwar interessant finde, wie ich alles Mögliche interessant finde, aber die Debatte kaum auch nur nachvollziehen, geschweige denn für meine Arbeit fruchtbar machen kann, und auch gar nicht den Drang dazu verspüre. ~~Ich bin gegenüber den allenthalben zu beobachtenden Versuchen, so etwas wie »Designtheorie« als Fach zu etablieren, ausgesprochen skeptisch.~~ Vielleicht reichen uns ja bewährte Begriffe wie »Urheberschaft« und »Gestaltungshöhe«?; die Letztere kennt den erfrischenden Nebenbegriff der »Kleinen Münze«, dem ich meine Arbeit gerne zurechne.

Planck-Anekdote nach Rolf Dobelli.

3.
Das heißt nicht, daß es zum Thema gar nichts zu sagen gäbe.

7

63

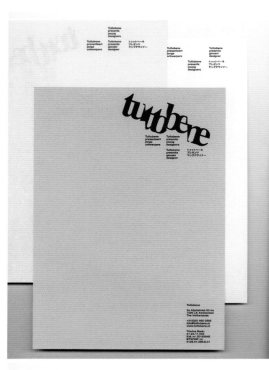

Typeface in Use
Times New Roman
Bold

"Tuttobene being a design organization we liked using the two archetypical fonts Times and Helvetica."

Tuttobene visual identity
2008 — Visual Identity
Client Tuttobene
Design Lesley Moore

Tuttobene is an organization which connects young designers with potential clients and manufacturers. This idea of connecting has been translated into a logo consisting only of ligatures. To reflect Tuttobene's sustainability approach, the stationery is printed on noncurrent paper which has been taken out of stock and otherwise would have been wasted.

Tuttobene
presents
young
designers

トゥットベーネ
プレゼンツ
ヤングデザイナー

Tuttobene
presenteert
jonge
ontwerpers

Tuttobene
presenta
giovani
designer

Tuttobene
presenteert
jonge
ontwerpers

Tuttobene
presenta
giovani
designer

Tuttobene
presents
young
designers

トゥットベーネ
プレゼンツ
ヤングデザイナー

Tuttobene

2e Atjehstraat 60-hs
1094 LK Amsterdam
The Netherlands

Tuttobene
presenteert
jonge
ontwerpers

Tuttobene
presents
young
designers

Tuttobene
presenta
giovani
designer

トゥットベーネ
プレゼンツ
ヤングデザイナー

The Tuttobene stationery is printed on non-current paper kindly provided by Grafisch Papier

Pieterjan Ginckels, S.P.A.M. BOOK
2011 — Editorial, Book Design
Client Be-Part
Design Jurgen Maelfeyt

Design in collaboration with the artist Pieterjan Ginckels. The book functions as a documentation and an object. The texture and color of the cover are exactly reconstructed from the wooden panels used in the installation. The book is now part of the performance/installation S.P.A.M. Office.

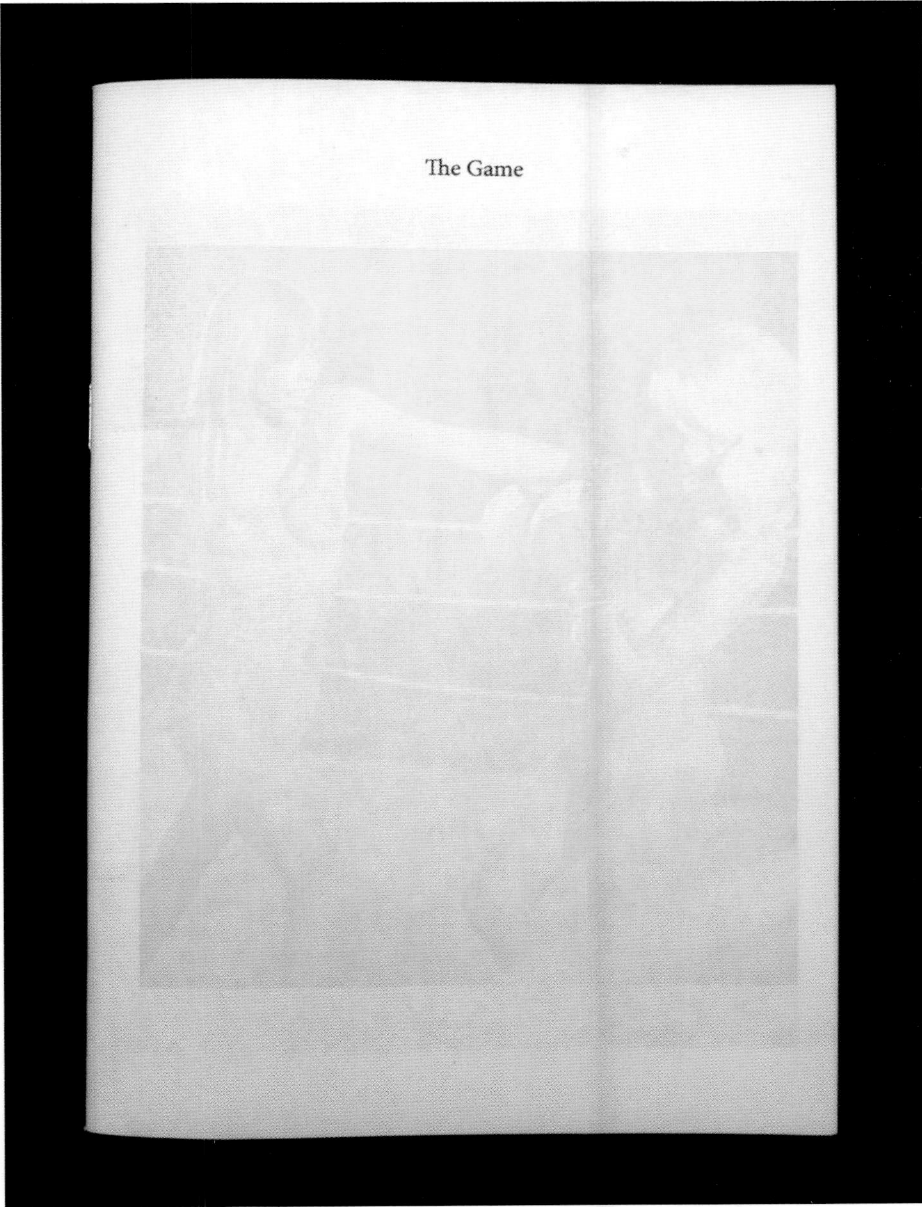

Jurgen Maelfeyt, The Game
2010 — Book Design
Design Jurgen Maelfeyt

Typeface in Use
Times

Artist book, printed with the Risograph GR 3770.

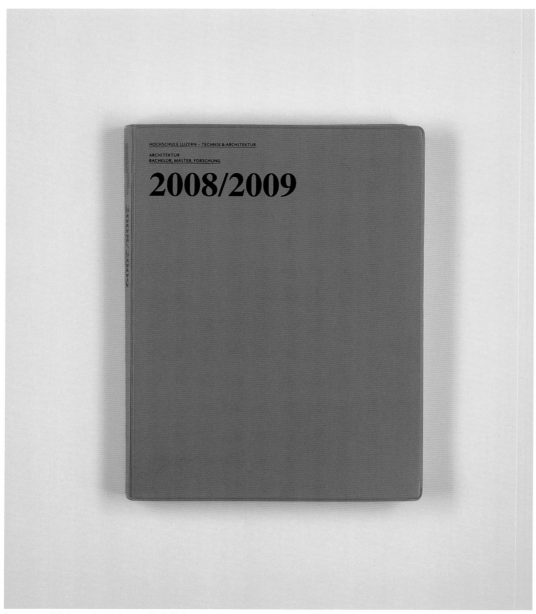

Lucerne University of Applied Sciences and Arts, Yearbook of the Architecture Department
2009 — Book Design
Client Lucerne University of Applied Sciences and Arts
Design Burri-Preis

Concept of the book was to make a reference book of students' work and the university's material archives, organized in formal categories like plans, images, text, materials. This shows in the structure of the book as well as in the cover material.

S

Burri-Preis' Favorite Times Letter is "S".

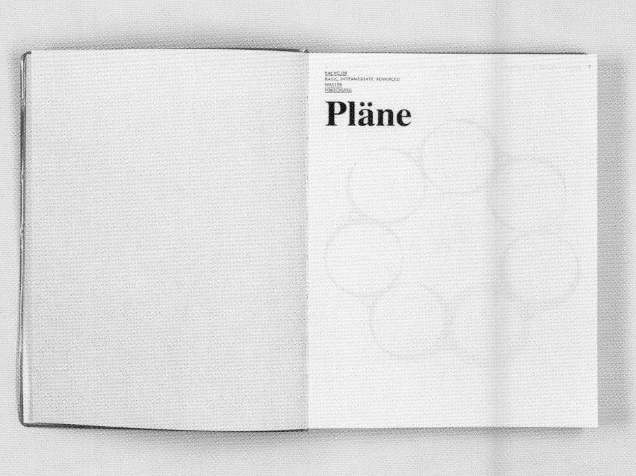

Typeface in Use
Times Regular,
Times Italic,
Times Bold,
FS Albert

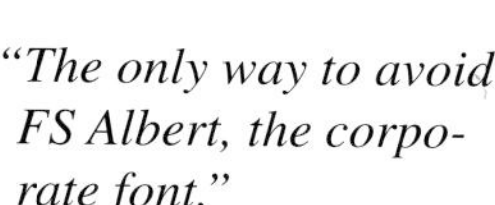

"The only way to avoid FS Albert, the corpo-rate font."

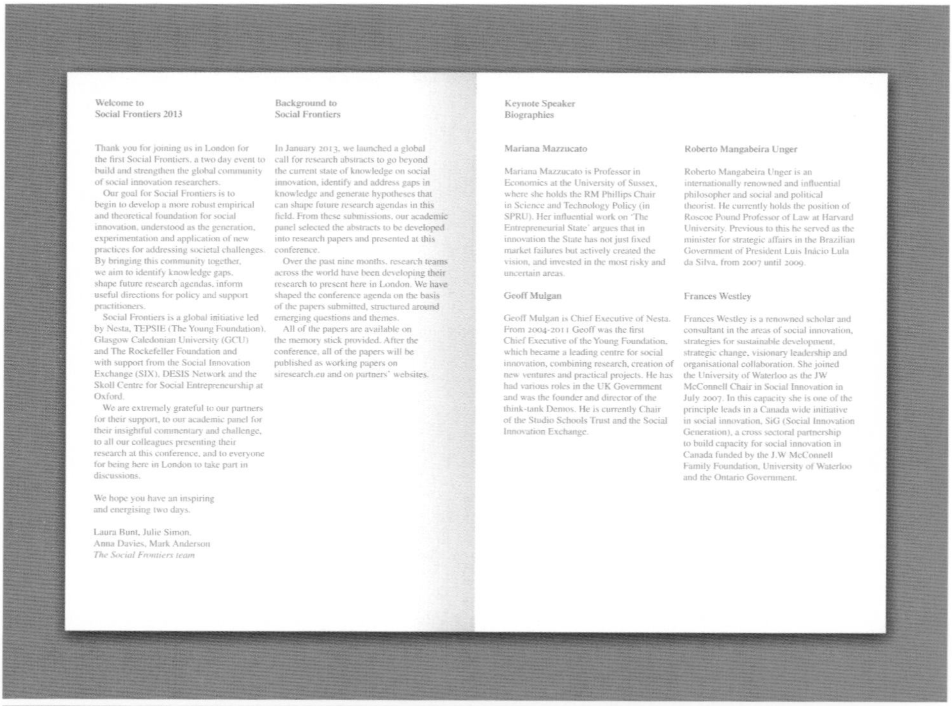

Welcome to Social Frontiers 2013

Thank you for joining us in London for the first Social Frontiers, a two day event to build and strengthen the global community of social innovation researchers.

Our goal for Social Frontiers is to begin to develop a more robust empirical and theoretical foundation for social innovation, understood as the generation, experimentation and application of new practices for addressing societal challenges. By bringing this community together, we aim to identify knowledge gaps, shape future research agendas, inform useful directions for policy and support practitioners.

Social Frontiers is a global initiative led by Nesta, TEPSIE (The Young Foundation), Glasgow Caledonian University (GCU) and The Rockefeller Foundation and with support from the Social Innovation Exchange (SIX), DESIS Network and the Skoll Centre for Social Entrepreneurship at Oxford.

We are extremely grateful to our partners for their support, to our academic panel for their insightful commentary and challenge, to all our colleagues presenting their research at this conference, and to everyone for being here in London to take part in discussions.

We hope you have an inspiring and energising two days.

Laura Bunt, Julie Simon,
Anna Davies, Mark Anderson
The Social Frontiers team

Background to Social Frontiers

In January 2013, we launched a global call for research abstracts to go beyond the current state of knowledge on social innovation, identify and address gaps in knowledge and generate hypotheses that can shape future research agendas in this field. From these submissions, our academic panel selected the abstracts to be developed into research papers and presented at this conference.

Over the past nine months, research teams across the world have been developing their research to present here in London. We have shaped the conference agenda on the basis of the papers submitted, structured around emerging questions and themes.

All of the papers are available on the memory stick provided. After the conference, all of the papers will be published as working papers on siresearch.eu and on partners' websites.

Keynote Speaker Biographies

Mariana Mazzucato

Mariana Mazzucato is Professor in Economics at the University of Sussex, where she holds the RM Phillips Chair in Science and Technology Policy (in SPRU). Her influential work on 'The Entrepreneurial State' argues that in innovation the State has not just fixed market failures but actively created the vision, and invested in the most risky and uncertain areas.

Geoff Mulgan

Geoff Mulgan is Chief Executive of Nesta. From 2004-2011 Geoff was the first Chief Executive of the Young Foundation, which became a leading centre for social innovation, combining research, creation of new ventures and practical projects. He has had various roles in the UK Government and was the founder and director of the think-tank Demos. He is currently Chair of the Studio Schools Trust and the Social Innovation Exchange.

Roberto Mangabeira Unger

Roberto Mangabeira Unger is an internationally renowned and influential philosopher and social and political theorist. He currently holds the position of Roscoe Pound Professor of Law at Harvard University. Previous to this he served as the minister for strategic affairs in the Brazilian Government of President Luis Inácio Lula da Silva, from 2007 until 2009.

Frances Westley

Frances Westley is a renowned scholar and consultant in the areas of social innovation, strategies for sustainable development, strategic change, visionary leadership and organisational collaboration. She joined the University of Waterloo as the JW McConnell Chair in Social Innovation in July 2007. In this capacity she is one of the principle leads in a Canada wide initiative in social innovation, SiG (Social Innovation Generation), a cross sectoral partnership to build capacity for social innovation in Canada funded by the J.W McConnell Family Foundation, University of Waterloo and the Ontario Government.

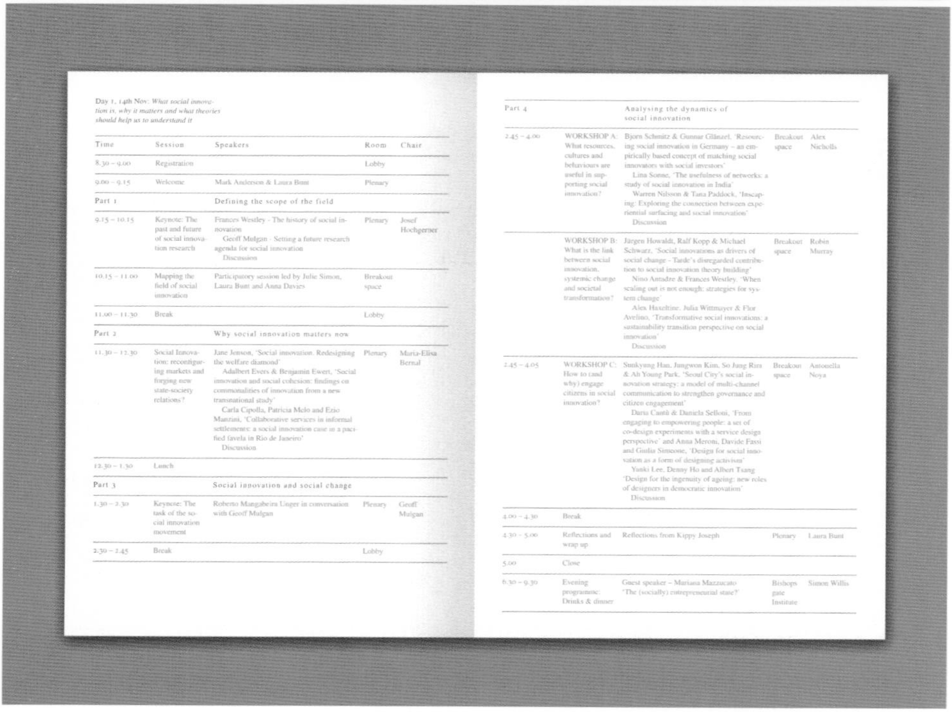

Day 1, 14th Nov: *What social innovation is, why it matters and what theories should help us to understand it*

Time	Session	Speakers	Room	Chair
8.30 – 9.00	Registration		Lobby	
9.00 – 9.15	Welcome	Mark Anderson & Laura Bunt	Plenary	
Part 1		Defining the scope of the field		
9.15 – 10.15	Keynote: The past and future of social innovation research	Frances Westley - The history of social innovation Geoff Mulgan - Setting a future research agenda for social innovation Discussion	Plenary	Josef Hochgerner
10.15 – 11.00	Mapping the field of social innovation	Participatory session led by Julie Simon, Laura Bunt and Anna Davies	Breakout space	
11.00 – 11.30	Break		Lobby	
Part 2		Why social innovation matters now		
11.30 – 12.30	Social Innovation: reconfiguring markets and forging new state-society relations?	Jane Jenson, 'Social innovation. Redesigning the welfare diamond' Adalbert Evers & Benjamin Ewert, 'Social innovation and social cohesion: findings on commonalities of innovation from a new transnational study' Carla Cipolla, Patricia Melo and Ezio Manzini, 'Collaborative services in informal settlements: a social innovation case in a pacified favela in Rio de Janeiro' Discussion	Plenary	Maria-Elisa Bernal
12.30 – 1.30	Lunch			
Part 3		Social innovation and social change		
1.30 – 2.30	Keynote: The task of the social innovation movement	Roberto Mangabeira Unger in conversation with Geoff Mulgan	Plenary	Geoff Mulgan
2.30 – 2.45	Break		Lobby	
Part 4		Analysing the dynamics of social innovation		
2.45 – 4.00	WORKSHOP A: What resources, cultures and behaviours are useful in supporting social innovation?	Bjorn Schmitz & Gunnar Glänzel, 'Resourcing social innovation in Germany – an empirically based concept of matching social innovators with social investors' Lina Sonne, 'The usefulness of networks: a study of social innovation in India' Warren Nilsson & Tana Paddock, 'Inscaping: Exploring the connection between experiential surfacing and social innovation' Discussion	Breakout space	Alex Nicholls
	WORKSHOP B: What is the link between social innovation, systemic change and societal transformation?	Jürgen Howaldt, Ralf Kopp & Michael Schwarz, 'Social innovations as drivers of social change - Tarde's disregarded contribution to social innovation theory building' Nino Antadze & Frances Westley, 'When scaling out is not enough: strategies for system change' Alex Haxeltine, Julia Wittmayer & Flor Avelino, 'Transformative social innovations: a sustainability transition perspective on social innovation' Discussion	Breakout space	Robin Murray
2.45 – 4.05	WORKSHOP C: How to (and why) engage citizens in social innovation?	Sunkyung Han, Jungwon Kim, So Jung Rim & Ah Young Park, 'Seoul City's social innovation strategy: a model of multi-channel communication to strengthen governance and citizen engagement' Daria Cantù & Daniela Selloni, 'From engaging to empowering people: a set of co-design experiments with a service design perspective' and Anna Meroni, Davide Fassi and Giulia Simeone, 'Design for social innovation as a form of designing activism' Yanki Lee, Denny Ho and Albert Tsang 'Design for the ingenuity of ageing: new roles of designers in democratic innovation' Discussion	Breakout space	Antonella Noya
4.00 – 4.30	Break			
4.30 – 5.00	Reflections and wrap up	Reflections from Kippy Joseph	Plenary	Laura Bunt
5.00	Close			
6.30 – 9.30	Evening programme: Drinks & dinner	Guest speaker – Mariana Mazzucato 'The (socially) entrepreneurial state?'	Bishops gate Institute	Simon Willis

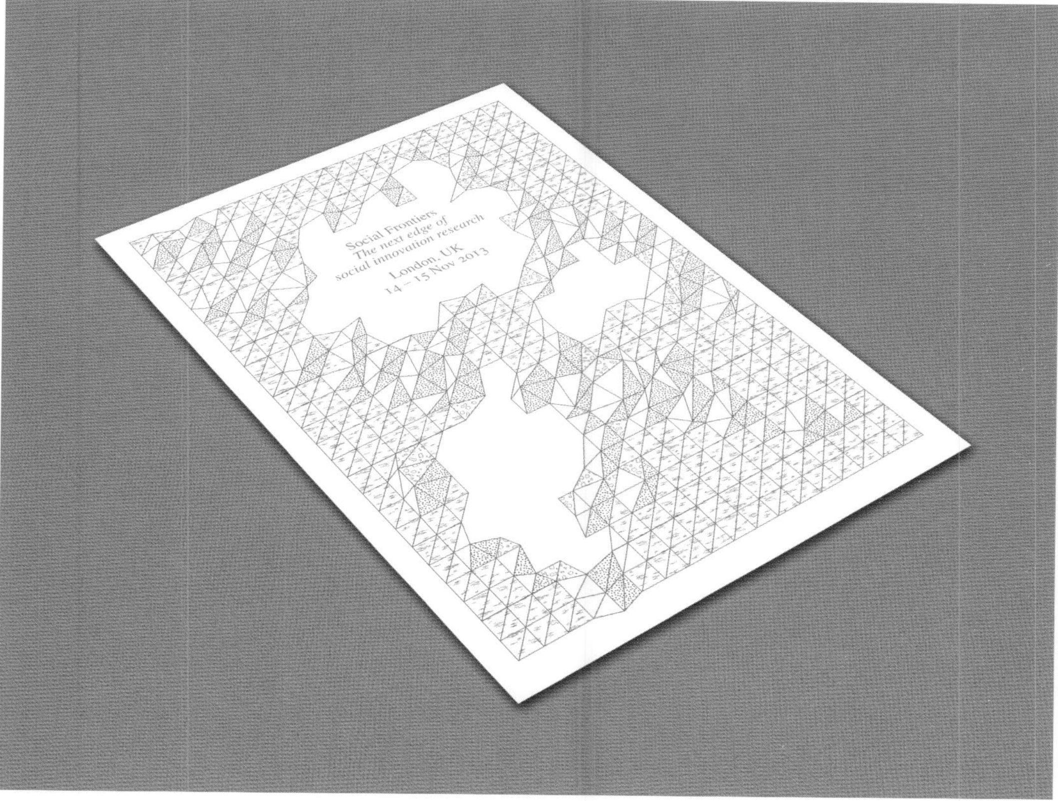

Social Frontiers:
The Next Edge of Social Innovation Research
2013 — Visual Identity
Client Nesta
Design TwoPoints.Net

Typeface in Use
Times LT Std

The global field of social innovation is gathering momentum. Yet despite thriving practitioner networks and a real commitment from policymakers and foundations to support social innovation, empirical and theoretical knowledge of social innovation remains uneven. Even though there are many organizations working in this field, much more could be done to bring these networks, organizations and individuals together.

This is the aim of Social Frontiers, to build and strengthen the community of social innovation researchers. By bringing together a multiplicity of voices and perspectives on social innovation we hope to strengthen and extend existing networks, share learning, promote collaboration, map out gaps in knowledge.

"Times helped to set the academic tone, being one of the most used typefaces in this field."

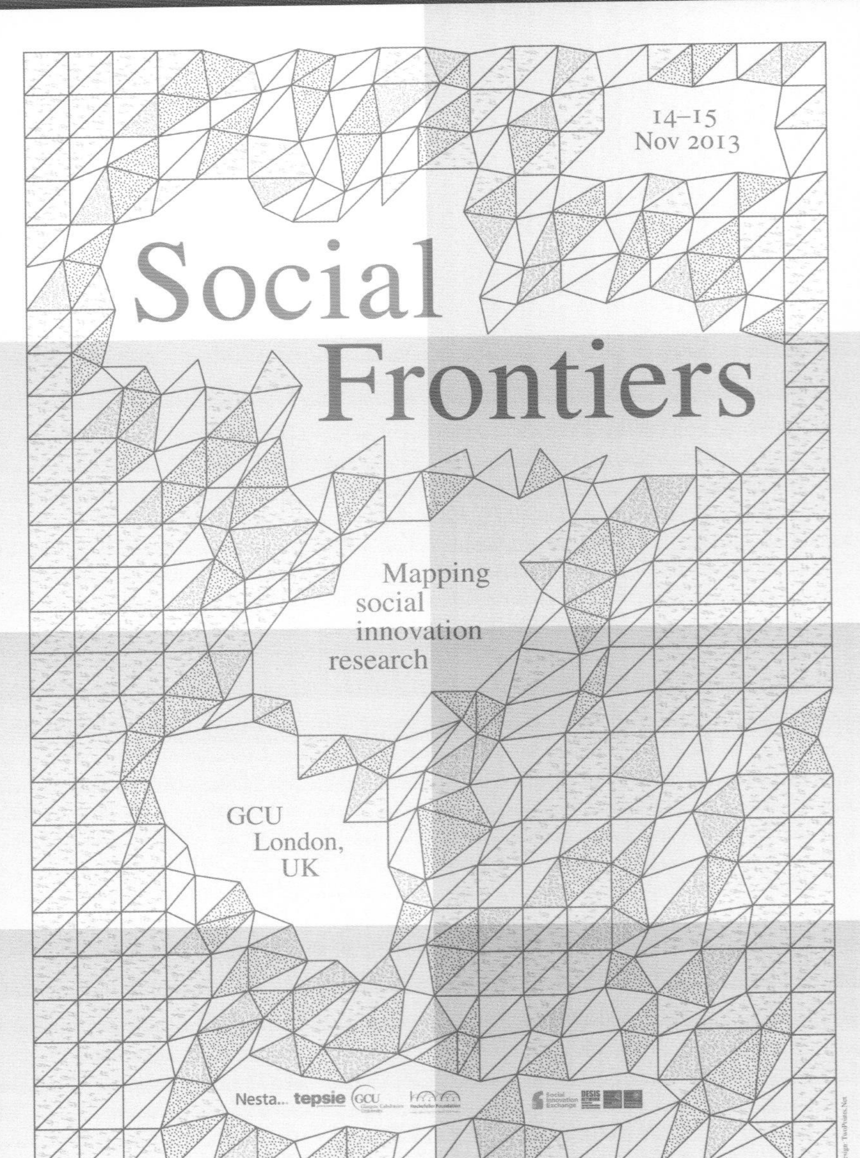
14–15
Nov 2013
Social
Frontiers
Mapping
social
innovation
research
GCU
London,
UK
Nesta...
tepsie
GCU
Social
Innovation
Exchange

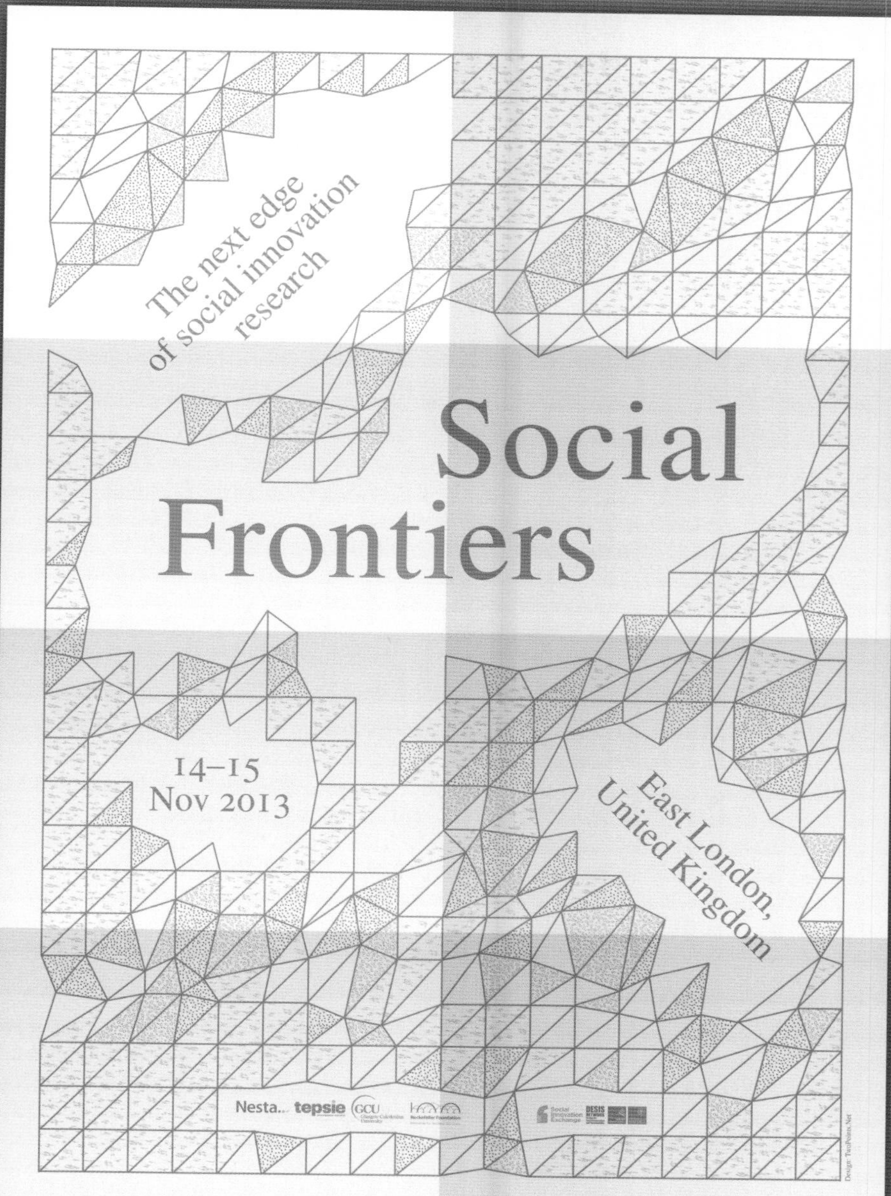
The next edge
of social innovation
research
Social
Frontiers
14–15
Nov 2013
East London,
United Kingdom
Nesta
tepsie
GCU
Social Innovation Exchange
DESIS
Design: TwoPoints.Net

1.1. Objectives

We hope to challenge traditional perceptions of advertising through creative innovation. The creative interpretations offered by Open Impact Channel will be placed in art venues, design symposia and art publications...

why? **Open Impact Channel believes your audience has changed.**

"In our culture, which has become a technological information culture, a high degree of 'visual literacy' has developed in large sections of the mass media audience… […] The content and effectiveness of communication have become strongly context-dependent, not least because the audience with whom the message communicates has itself matured."

Max Bruinsma, 1999
(Max Bruinsma is an independent Dutch writer, curator, editor and design critic)

10

Analysis:

**Your audience is not stupid!
Effectiveness is context-dependent**

Result:

The advertising world strongly underestimates the public.

Conclusion:

The context influences your message!

Solution!

Open Impact Channel wants to negate the current situation by offering new perspectives within the advertising industry. By offering new advertising carriers and by creating original and unique advertising 'tools', we hope to set new standards in a business which has become self-indulgent. We offer a brand new dimension within advertising!

11

1.2. Mission

Open Impact Channel is a strategic communications company dedicated exclusively to the invention of alternative advertising programs for commercial brands. The sole business purpose is to provide a new avenue of promotional effectiveness for your brand so you can get more attention from your customers. The public space is our playground, we go for:

- Maximum exposure
- Maximum impact
- Honest, open communication
- Public development
- Public satisfaction
- 0% Carbon footprint
- Participation
- Cooperation
- Teamwork
- Creativity and innovation
- Resource efficiency
- Prudent risk-taking

14

1.3. Keys To Success

**Your limit?
Our imagination!**

We believe success is measured by maintaining the highest standards of integrity in every action we take and in everything we do. We take the highest account on the intellectual independency of our art public. We offer valuable, mature solutions grounded upon creativity and innovation.

**360°
visibility
100%
impact**

15

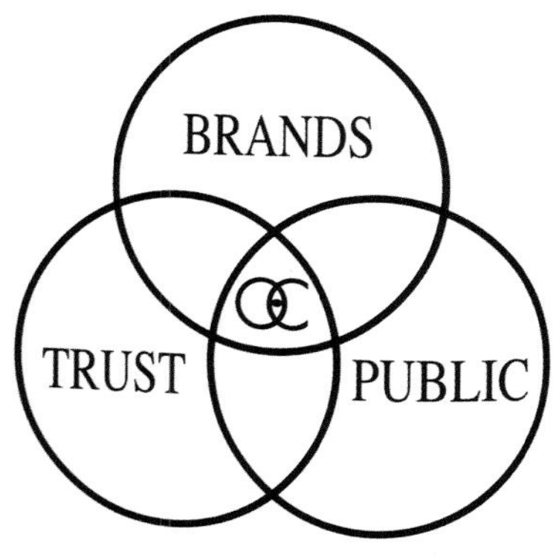

2.1. Industry Expertise
Excellence in fulfilling the promise to grow the relationship with your brand through confidential, reliable expertise and trustworthy execution, is our prime goal.
Trust is the key word for good business relationships!
BRANDS
TRUST
PUBLIC
24
For Open Impact Channel, a good relationship with your brand is important, but the relationship with your public is of greater importance.
PROBLEMS?
SOLUTIONS!
We see it as our mission to reconcile the relationship between brands and the artistic audience!
25

Open Impact Channel
2010 — Book Design
Design Cox & Grusenmeyer

Open Impact Channel is an imaginary advertising company that explores the ethics and rhetorical aspects of a corporate enterprise. The Open Impact Channel Business Plan is the core summary of the OIC strategy. By means of a strict choreography and a strong visual language the reader is fluently guided through the envisioned plans of the company. The content is a mash-up of other business plans with typical slogans and advertising lingo. The bombastic design of the slightly oversized book extrapolates simplistic reasonings into straight forward diagrams, convincing promises, hollow words and pseudo-scientific facts.

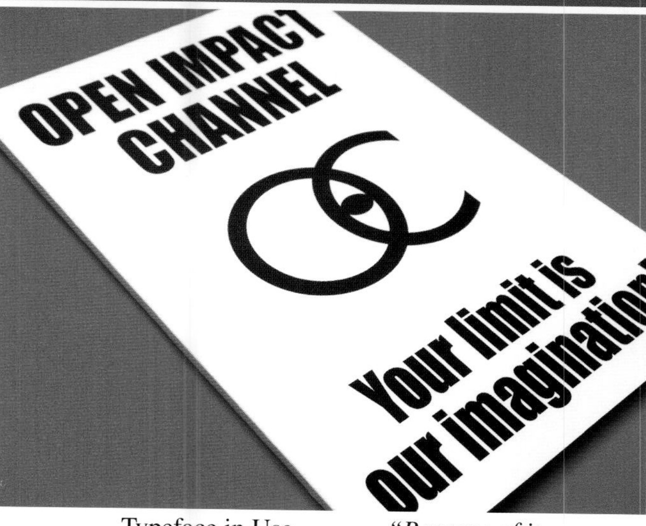

Typeface in Use
Customized Times, Impact

"Because of its 'default' character."

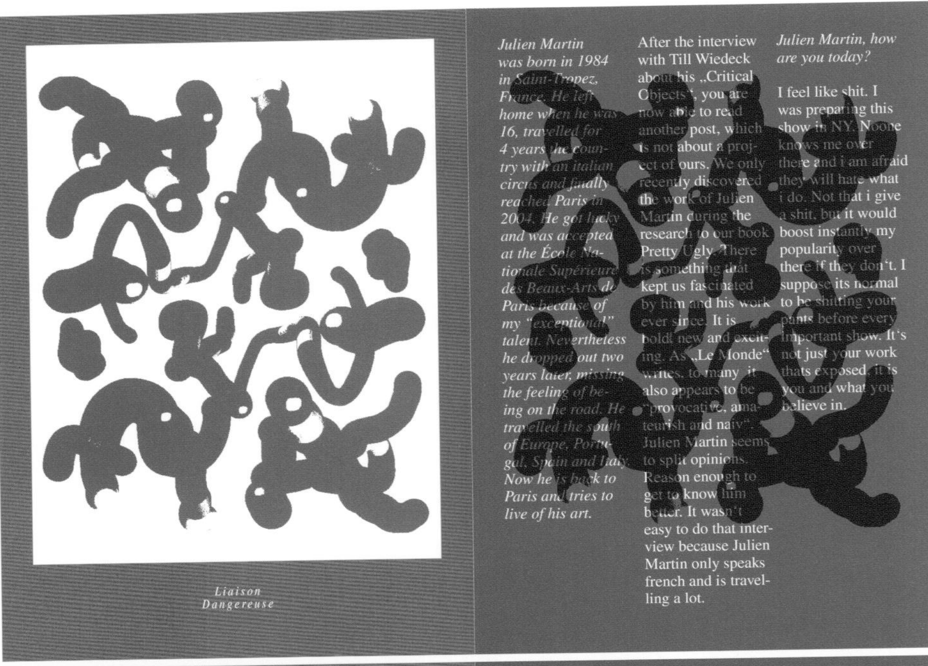

Liaison
Dangereuse
Julien Martin was born in 1984 in Saint-Tropez, France. He left home when he was 16, travelled for 4 years the country with an italian circus and finally reached Paris in 2004. He got lucky and was accepted at the École Nationale Supérieure des Beaux-Arts de Paris because of my "exceptional" talent. Nevertheless he dropped out two years later, missing the feeling of being on the road. He travelled the south of Europe, Portugal, Spain and Italy. Now he is back to Paris and tries to live of his art.
After the interview with Till Wiedeck about his „Critical Objects", you are now able to read another post, which is not about a project of ours. We only recently discovered the work of Julien Martin during the research to our book Pretty Ugly. There is something that kept us fascinated by him and his work ever since. It is bold, new and exciting. As „Le Monde" writes, to many it also appears to be "provocative, amateurish and naiv". Julien Martin seems to split opinions. Reason enough to get to know him better. It wasn't easy to do that interview because Julien Martin only speaks french and is travelling a lot.
Julien Martin, how are you today?
I feel like shit. I was preparing this show in NY. Noone knows me over there and i am afraid they will hate what i do. Not that i give a shit, but it would boost instantly my popularity over there if they don't. I suppose its normal to be shitting your pants before every important show. It's not just your work thats exposed, it is you and what you believe in.

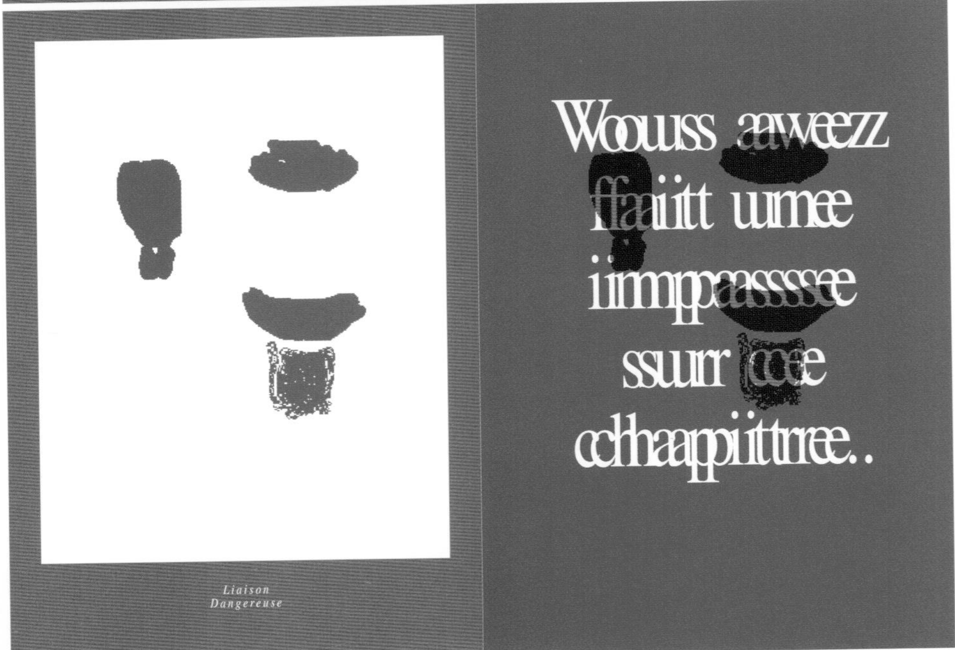

Typeface in Use
Times LT Std

"The work of Julien Martin required a typeface that's both classy and 'default'. Times embraces both concepts."

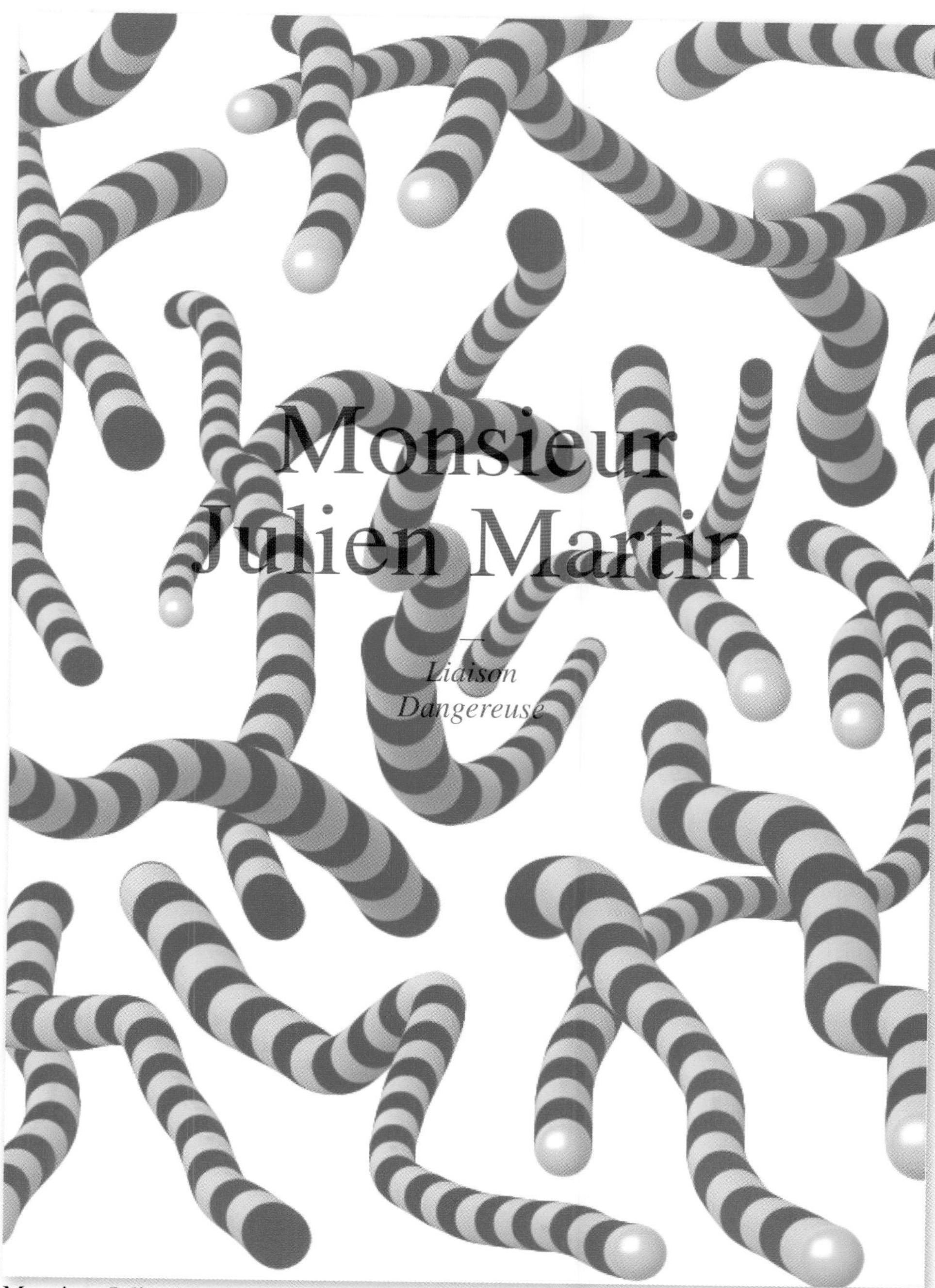

Monsieur Julien Martin — Liaison Dangereuse 2012 — Publication Design MJM

Art catalog for French artist Monsieur Julien Martin's first exhibition.

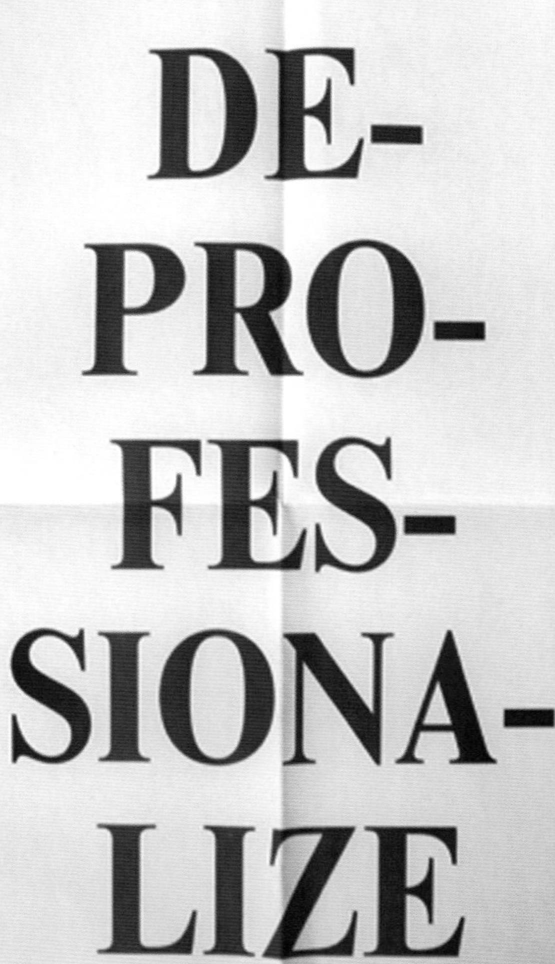

DEPROFESSIONALIZE
2010 — Poster
Client David Horvitz
Design Mylinh Trieu Nguyen

DEPROFESSIONALIZE. A suggestion, a statement, a reminder, a mantra, a life-style, a choice. The design of this poster focuses on the articulation of these things, literally and figuratively, forcing the enunciation of each syllable, while committing hyphenation crime.

D
raw
ing
that
changes
the
world,
Seoul
2012

세상을
바꾸는
드로잉
2012
서울

WORDS
ARE FLOWING OUT
LIKE
ENDLESS RAIN

THEY
SLIP AWAY
ACROSS THE UNIVERSE.

JAI
GURU
DEVA
OM

NOTHING'S
GONNA CHANGE
MY WORLD

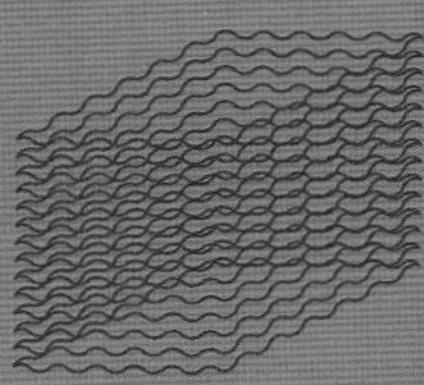

언어는
끝없는 비처럼
흘러

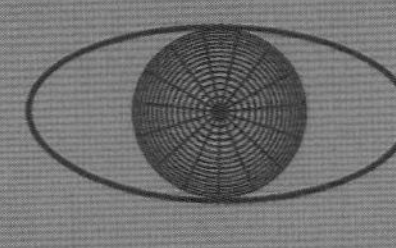

우주
저편으로
사라지고

JAI
GURU
DEVA
OM

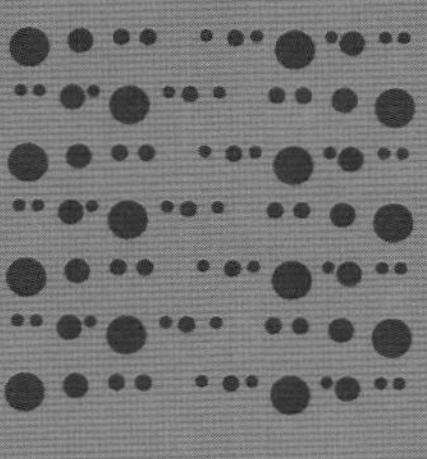

'아무
것도
아닌
것'
만이
나의

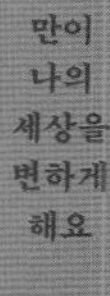

세상을
변하게
해요

THE BEATLES,
<ACROSS THE UNIVERSE>

TAKEOUT DRAWING

DESIGN · TYPEPAGE / www.typepage.com

Takeout Drawing Invitation Card
2012 — Invitation Card
Client Cutural Space, Takeout Drawing
Design TypePage (Jin Dallae, Park Woohyuk)

The invitation card for the opening of new site of Takeout Drawing.

Typeface in Use
Times New Roman Bold

"Times New Roman is one of the most neutral typefaces but has a classic and modern appearance at the same time. Takeout Drawing is a space where every cultural event is possible. So, for that space, we decided to use the typeface 'Times New Roman' as the typeface makes every expression possible."

Jan

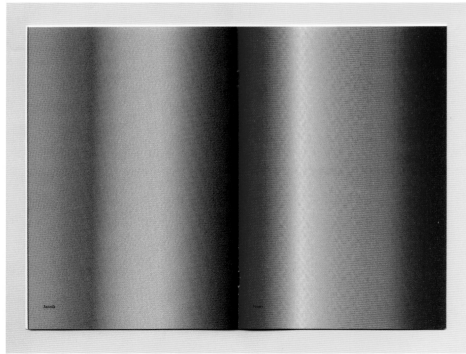
Jannik
Jenny

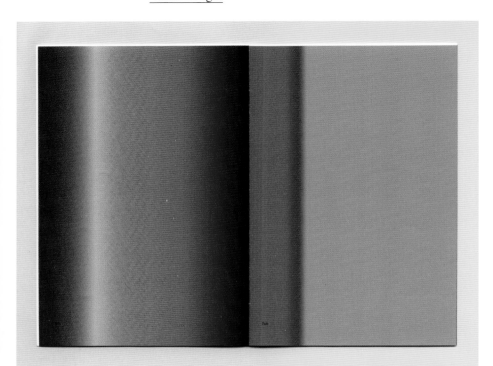

Visual Aspects of Synaesthesia
2012 — Booklet
Design Burri-Preis

Self-initiated visual research project on the topic of grapheme color synaesthesia and number forms.

A–Z A–Z A–Z A–Z

WELCHE FARBE HAT EIN S?

A–Z A–Z A–Z –Z

A–Z A–Z A– A–Z

A– –Z A–Z A–Z

–Z A–Z A–Z A–Z

A–Z A–Z Burri-Preis A–Z A–Z

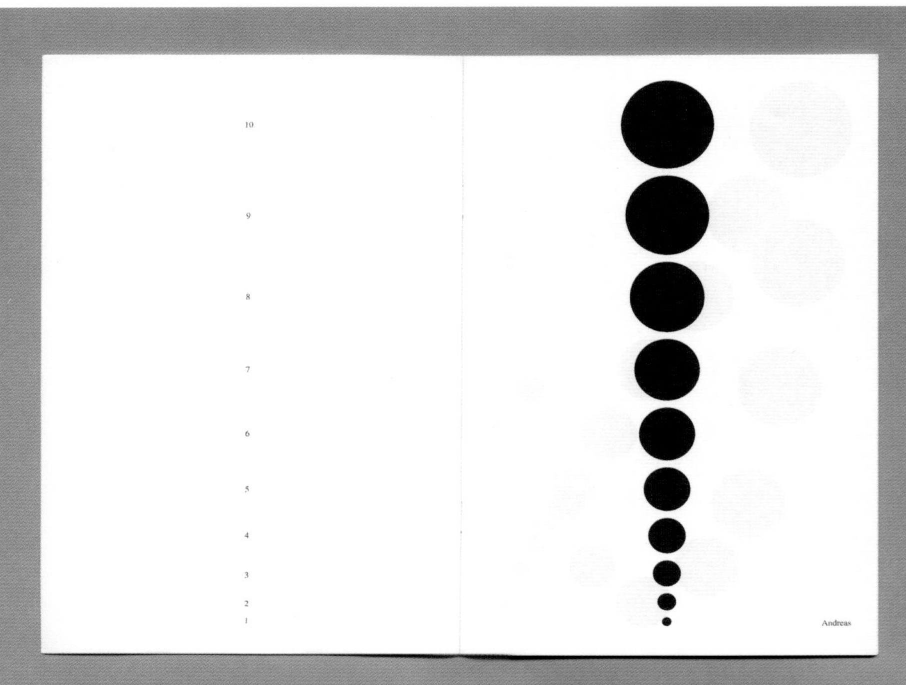
10
9
8
7
6
5
4
3
2
1
Andreas

Jannik
Magnus

Typeface in Use
Times Regular,
Times Bold

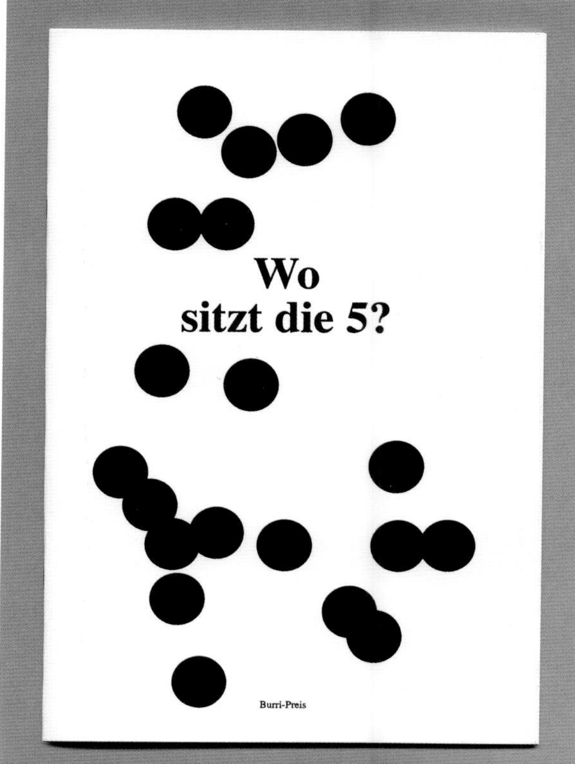

"In these publications we wanted the synaesthetic visualizations to be in the center of attention. So we used Times as a quite quiet and common, but still very beautiful typeface."

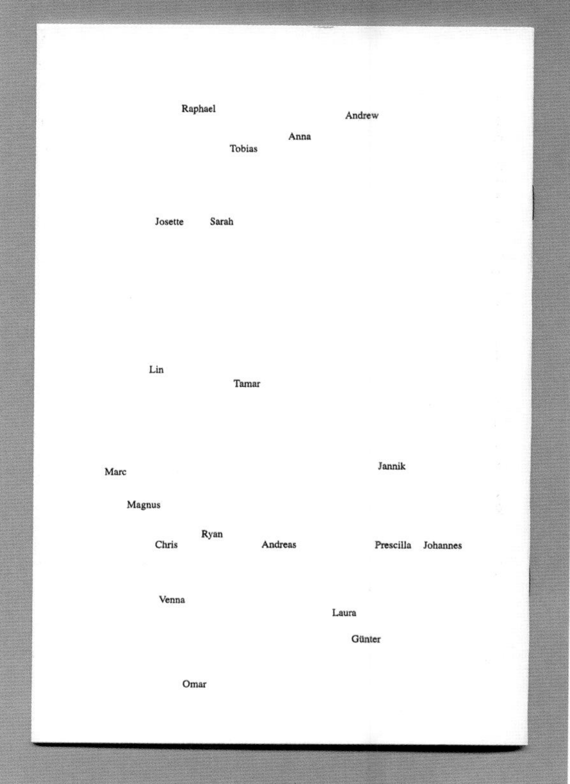

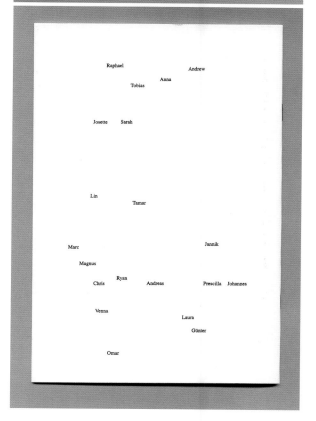

Diplomarbeit im Fachbereich Mal- und Kunsttherapie am IAC Zürich

von Marion Bernegger
Ausbildung 2004 – 2007, Abgabe März 2009
Leitung: Bruno Wirth

Maltherapie mit den vergessenen Kindern von Addis Abeba/ Æthiopien

Marion Bernegger, Nürenbergstrasse 10, 8037 Zürich.
marion.bernegger@gmx.net

1

Es war auch packend, wie sich die Kinder mit Ursli identifizierten und die Geschichte ohne gross nachzudenken reflektierten und auch ihre Gefühle darüber zum Ausdruck brachten. Sie begriffen, dass Ursli mutig und clever genug war, aus der kurzen Hoffnungslosigkeit heraus, die Initiative zu ergreifen und dass er sich auf den Weg gemacht hatte, um diese Glocke zu holen und somit sein Problem zu lösen.

Zum Abschluss gab es an diesem Nachmittag noch eine kleine Überraschung für die tapferen Kinder. Ich hatte aus der Schweiz kleine, goldige Glöcklein mitgebracht und wollte ihnen diese als Andenken und als Glücksbringer mit auf den Weg geben. Die strahlenden Kinderaugen und ihre offenherzige Dankbarkeit werde ich für ein Leben lang in meinem Herzen tragen.

In den nächsten Tagen hörte man die vielen äthiopischen Schellen-Urslis draussen auf 2500 Metern über Meer glöckeln. Ich hatte nicht mit solch einer Freude der Kinder gerechnet und vor allem nicht damit, dass kurz darauf alle anderen auch solche kleine Glocken haben wollten. Zum guten Glück hatte ich noch diverse Holzperlen und Buchstaben aus Kunstmaterial mit eingepackt und somit bekam jeder der wollte eine Halskette mit den gewünschten Anhängern.

Einschub: Folgende Kanäle können durch Geschichten erzählen [illegible] werden:
Die Hörfähigkeit: [illegible]
Die Konzentration: Hochmotiviertes Zuhören ist eng verwandt mit gesteigerter Konzentration. [illegible]
Grundvertrauen: Erzählen und Hören von Geschichten ist tief greifende Kommunikation. [illegible]
Wertvorstellungen und Weltanschauung: Märchen, Geschichten und Erzählungen sind durchdrungen von Wertvorstellungen [illegible]
(Quelle: Michael Schnabel, Wissenschaftlicher Angestellter am Staatsinstitut für Frühpädagogik)

Auch die Geschichte von Malwida, der Königin der Farben, wurde von den Kindern einverleibt und sie malten im Anschluss an das Erzählen das Schloss der Königin aus ihrer eigenen Phantasie und nach ihren Wünschen. Ich kopierte

56

ihnen eine weisse Vorlage des Schlosses und voller Elan malten sie diese Vorlage kunterbunt und kreativ aus.

Auch «Der kleine Prinz» (Originaltitel: Le Petit Prince), die illustrierte Erzählung von Antoine de Saint-Exupéry kam nun auch in Addis Abeba an. Die Geschichte ist ein modernes Märchen, das sowohl Erwachsene als auch Kinder anspricht. Es stellt ein Plädoyer für Freundschaft und Menschlichkeit dar.

Leider hatte ich keine Zeit mehr, mit diesem Buch anzufangen. Ich hatte dies jedoch dem Psychologen Dires übergeben, in der Hoffnung, dass er mit dem Geschichten erzählen fortfahren möge. Denn auch diese Geschichte, sowie die Illustrationen, werden die Phantasie und die Kreativität der Kinder bestimmt anregen.

**Man sieht nur mit dem Herzen gut.
Das Wesentliche ist für die Augen unsichtbar.**

Der kleine Prinz

Dies ist ein willkommenes Schlusszitat für dieses Kapitel. Während meiner intensiven Arbeit mit den Strassenkindern von *Sport – The Bridge* in Addis Abeba haben genau diese Kinder mir gezeigt, wie man mit dem Herzen sehen kann.

Wir schauen hauptsächlich mit den Augen. Augen und Verstand interpretieren, sie urteilen und vor allem beurteilen sie, ständig und zu jedem Augenblick. Das Herz jedoch ist unabhängig von persönlichen, visuellen Wahrnehmungen. Diese Kinder haben trotz allem, was sie mit ihren Augen bereits sehen und erleben mussten, nicht verlernt, mit dem Herzen zu schauen.

Und genau deren Sichtweise hat mich täglich, trotz all den vielen Widerständen wieder zum Aufstehen und Weitermachen bewogen, hat mir die Kraft und den Willen verliehen, einen neuen Tag in dieser für das Auge kaum vorstellbaren Stadt anzugehen und durchzustehen.
Ich musste meine Augen so oft verschliessen, damit mein Herz all diese vielen, unfassbaren Eindrücke und Augenblicke einigermassen ertragen konnte.

57

Burri-Preis' Favorite Times Letter is "E".

"To document the experience of painting therapy during this certain period we used this classical newspaper-typeface."

Typeface in Use
Times

Marion Bernegger, Documentation of Painting Therapy with the Forgotten Children of Addis Abeba
2009 — Book, Thesis
Client Marion Bernegger
Design Burri-Preis

Warum Äthiopien? – Einleitung

Absicht und Entstehung meiner Konzeptidee
Ja, es gibt sie doch!
Durch die Kollekte an der Hochzeit meiner Cousine Anja, Ende September 2007, bekam ich die «himmlische Eingebung», mit Strassenkindern in Addis Abeba zu arbeiten. Die Spendensammlung in der Kirche ging an das Projekt *Sport – The Bridge* in Äthiopien und für mich war plötzlich klar, wovon meine Diplomarbeit handeln würde. Voller Freude über diese «Erleuchtung» verliess ich die Kirche und stiess noch am selben Abend auf den Initiator des Projektes. Ich informierte ihn über meine Idee und fragte ihn, wie eine Umsetzung aussehen könnte.

Durch den Gründer Stephan Zihler kannte ich das Projekt schon von Beginn an und durch unser Wiedersehen an dieser Hochzeit Ende September 2007 kam mir die Idee, die Strassenkinder von *Sport – The Bridge* übers Malen zu begleiten und meine Diplomarbeit über das Erfahrene und Erlebte zu schreiben.

Ich wollte die mir am Ausbildungsinstitut *IAC* vermittelten gestalterischen/künstlerischen als auch psychologischen und pädagogischen Kenntnisse direkt anwenden und auswerten. Das Ausdrucksmalen mit den Strassenkindern in Addis Abeba würde einen wichtigen Teil meines Einsatzes im Projekt *Sport – The Bridge* einnehmen.

Lässt sich die Maltherapie, wie sie mir am *IAC* (Integratives Ausbildungsinstitut, Zürich) vermittelt wurde, im Rahmen des Projektes *Sport – The Bridge* in Äthiopien umsetzen und können meine bisherigen Erfahrungen dadurch erweitert werden? Ist es überhaupt denkbar, die Strassenkinder von Addis Abeba über diese Art von Malen zu erreichen?

Vorbereitungen in der Schweiz
Ende Dezember 2007 bekam ich die Zusage von den Verantwortlichen in Bern. Voller Vorfreude und auch einer unvermeidlichen Nervosität ging es an die sorgfältigen Vorbereitungen. Die Reisevorbereitungs-Checkliste wurde mir vom Projekt zugestellt, und da hiess es unter anderem, dass folgende Impfungen gemacht werden müssen: Gelbfieber, Typhus abdominalis, Hepatitis A/B, Tollwut, Meningokokken-Meningitis, Diphterie, Tetanus, Poliomyelitis, Malaria Prophylaxe, div. Kinderkrankheiten wie MMR (Masern-Mumps-Röteln) sowie Varizellen (Windpocken).

Und die Reaktion meiner beratenden Tropenärztin war eindeutig: WARUM ÄTHIOPIEN? Als ich dann diese vielen Impfungen schwarz auf weiss vor mir hatte, wurde es mir doch das erste Mal ganz mulmig und ich habe mich ernsthaft gefragt, was ich hier eigentlich genau mache.

Ich liess mich aber von zusätzlichen Unfall- und Krankenversicherungen, Visabeantragung, Rega-Mitgliedschaft, Informationen über Krankheiten bei den Kindern und von Berichten über den Zustand des Landes nicht abschrecken.

Obwohl mir immer bewusster wurde, worauf ich mich hier Ende Dezember 2007 eingelassen hatte, war der Wunsch, mit diesen Kindern und diesem Land in Kontakt zu treten, um einiges stärker, als die Angst und die Zweifel, die mich auch immer wieder heimsuchten.

Somit verbrachte ich die Zeit von Anfang Januar 2008 bis zu meiner Abreise am 9. April 2008 mit Vorbereitungen persönlicher und auch fachlicher Art.

4

«Denn es war ja so: Nelio war nicht nur ein armes, schmutziges Strassenkind gewesen. Er war vor allem ein bemerkenswerter Mensch, ungreifbar, vieldeutig, wie ein seltener Vogel, von dem alle reden, obwohl ihn niemand je wirklich gesehen hat. Obwohl er erst zehn Jahre alt war, als er starb, verfügte er über eine Erfahrung und Lebensweisheit, als hätte er hundert Jahre gelebt…
Und jetzt war Nelio tot.
Tief im Fieber versunken hatte er mühsam seinen letzten Atemzug ausgeschwitzt. Eine einsame Dünung hatte sich über die Weltmeere fortgepflanzt, dann war alles vorüber, und die Stille erschreckend in ihrer Leere. Ich sah zum Firmament auf und dachte, nichts würde mehr so sein, wie es war...
Es ist nicht, weil ich Angst habe, man könne mich vergessen, hatte er gesagt. Es ist, damit ihr nicht vergesst, wer ihr selber seid.»

Zeilen aus Chronist der Winde/Henning Mankell

5

Fluisterhappening (Whisperhappening)
2009 — Brochure
Client Concerttgebouw Brugge
Design Jurgen Maelfeyt

Typeface in Use
Times, Avenir

Program design for a happening about silence.

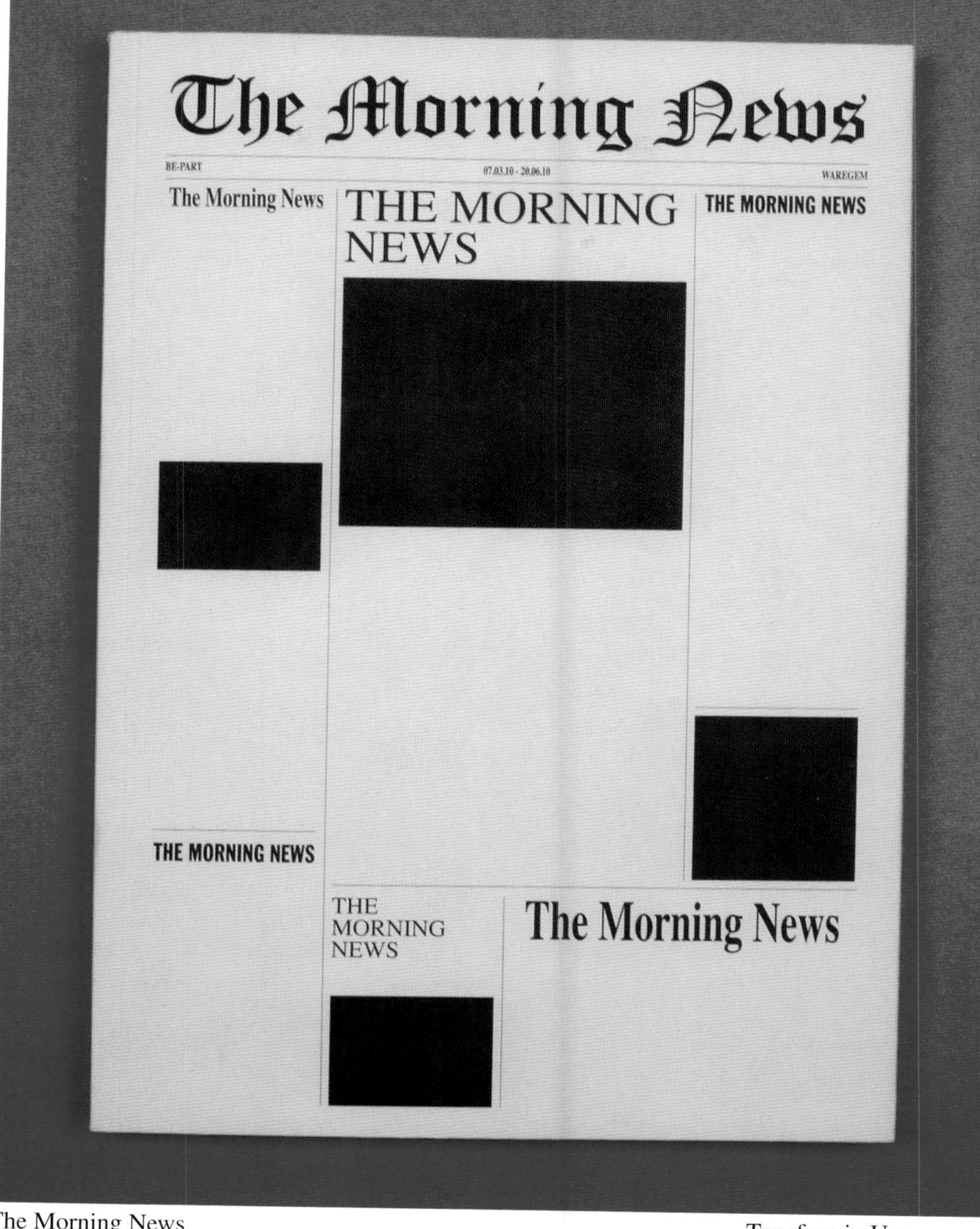

The Morning News
2010 — Catalog
Client Be-Part
Design Jurgen Maelfeyt

Typeface in Use
Times,
Old English text,
Franklin Gothic

Catalog design for exhibition 'The Morning News'. One of the artists (Brian Clifton) was never at the exhibition but only contributed in the catalog. The book was first designed as a 'regular' catalog and then we exchanged PDFs integrating his interventions.

What is the ultimate form of communication, and will we ever get there?

The simple information search days are numbered.

Knowledge is the library's commodity.

Can libraries be franchised?

Libraries are in the knowledge business.

THE ARCHITECTURE OF KNOWLEDGE.

"Times New Roman is one of the most widely used typefaces in book typography history. We choose the Times New Roman for the reason of its randomness — we wanted to use a typeface that everybody would be able to recognize."

Typeface in Use
Times Roman

The Architecture of Knowledge.
The library of the future.
2009 — Campaign
Client Netherlands Architecture Institute
Design Stout/Kramer

'The architecture of knowledge. The public library of the future.' is a collaborative project organized by The Netherlands Public Library Association and the Netherlands Architecture Institute (NAI), consisting of a lecture series followed by a two-week workshop for students. Information is knowledge. Knowledge is the library's commodity. As a result it attracts producers and consumers of this knowledge. To survive it should be aware and adaptable to changes and influences in this age of information and communication. What form and position will its physical and conceptual structure need to take in order to endure these changes in the data saturated realm of public and private society?

The campaign consists of small posters asking questions about the future role of the library in our society. The posters are like teasers for the event. Just to start a discussion about the subject. The final poster is a poster containing all the information of the event.

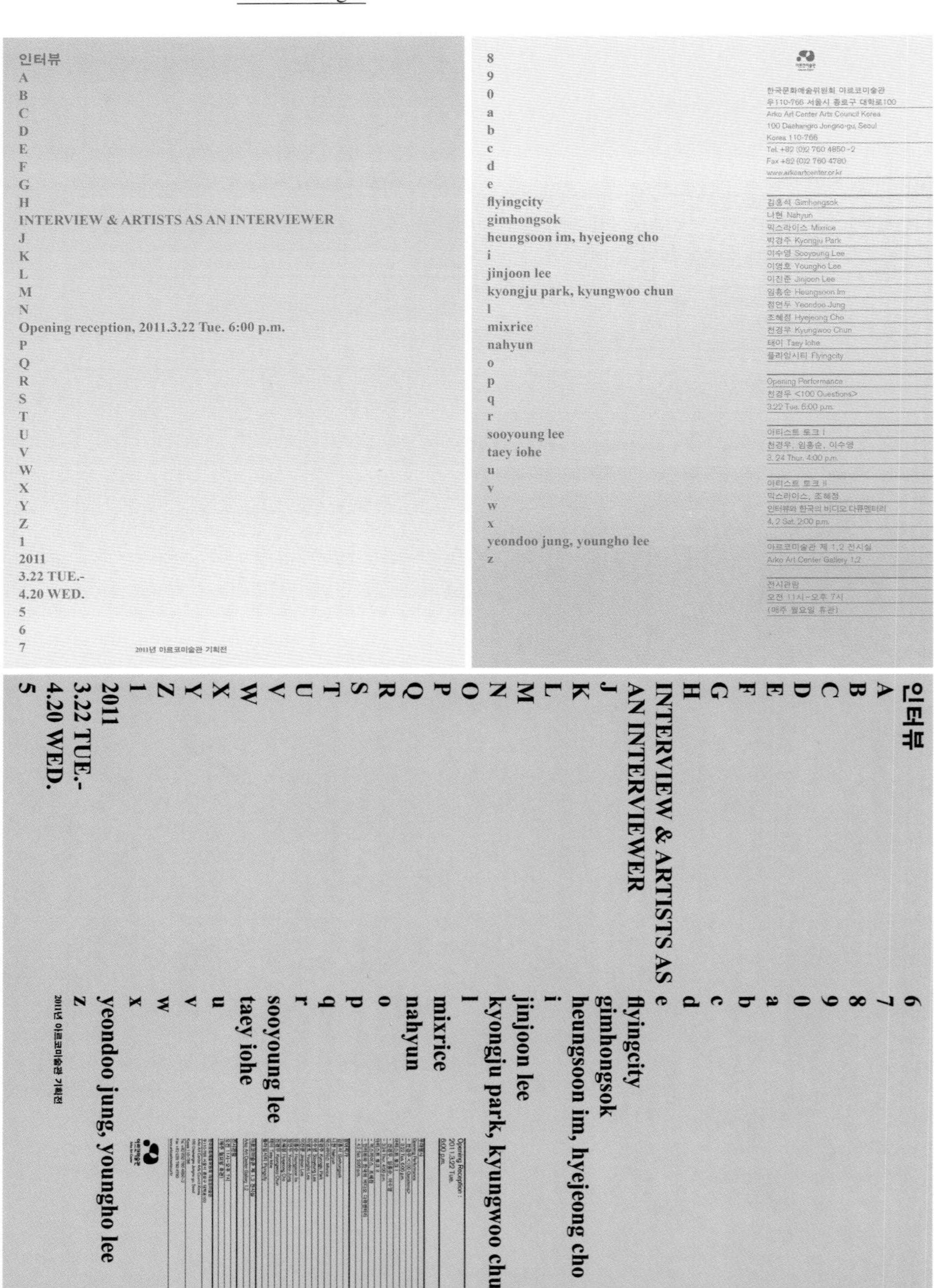
인터뷰
A
B
C
D
E
F
G
H
INTERVIEW & ARTISTS AS AN INTERVIEWER
J
K
L
M
N
Opening reception, 2011.3.22 Tue. 6:00 p.m.
P
Q
R
S
T
U
V
W
X
Y
Z
1
2011
3.22 TUE.-
4.20 WED.
5
6
7
2011년 아르코미술관 기획전
8
9
0
a
b
c
d
e
flyingcity
gimhongsok
heungsoon im, hyejeong cho
i
jinjoon lee
kyongju park, kyungwoo chun
l
mixrice
nahyun
o
p
q
r
sooyoung lee
taey iohe
u
v
w
x
yeondoo jung, youngho lee
z
한국문화예술위원회 아르코미술관
우110-766 서울시 종로구 대학로100
Arko Art Center Arts Council Korea
100 Daehangro Jongno-gu, Seoul
Korea 110-766
Tel. +82 (0)2 760 4850~2
Fax +82 (0)2 760 4780
www.arkoartcenter.or.kr
김홍석 Gimhongsok
나현 Nahyun
믹스라이스 Mixrice
박경주 Kyongju Park
이수영 Sooyoung Lee
이영호 Youngho Lee
이진준 Jinjoon Lee
임흥순 Heungsoon Im
정연두 Yeondoo Jung
조혜정 Hyejeong Cho
천경우 Kyungwoo Chun
태이 Taey Iohe
플라잉시티 Flyingcity
Opening Performance
천경우 <100 Questions>
3.22 Tue. 6:00 p.m.
아티스트 토크 I
천경우, 임흥순, 이수영
3. 24 Thur. 4:00 p.m.
아티스트 토크 II
믹스라이스, 조혜정
인터뷰와 한국의 비디오 다큐멘터리
4. 2 Sat. 2:00 p.m.
아르코미술관 제 1,2 전시실
Arko Art Center Gallery 1,2
전시관람
오전 11시~오후 7시
(매주 월요일 휴관)

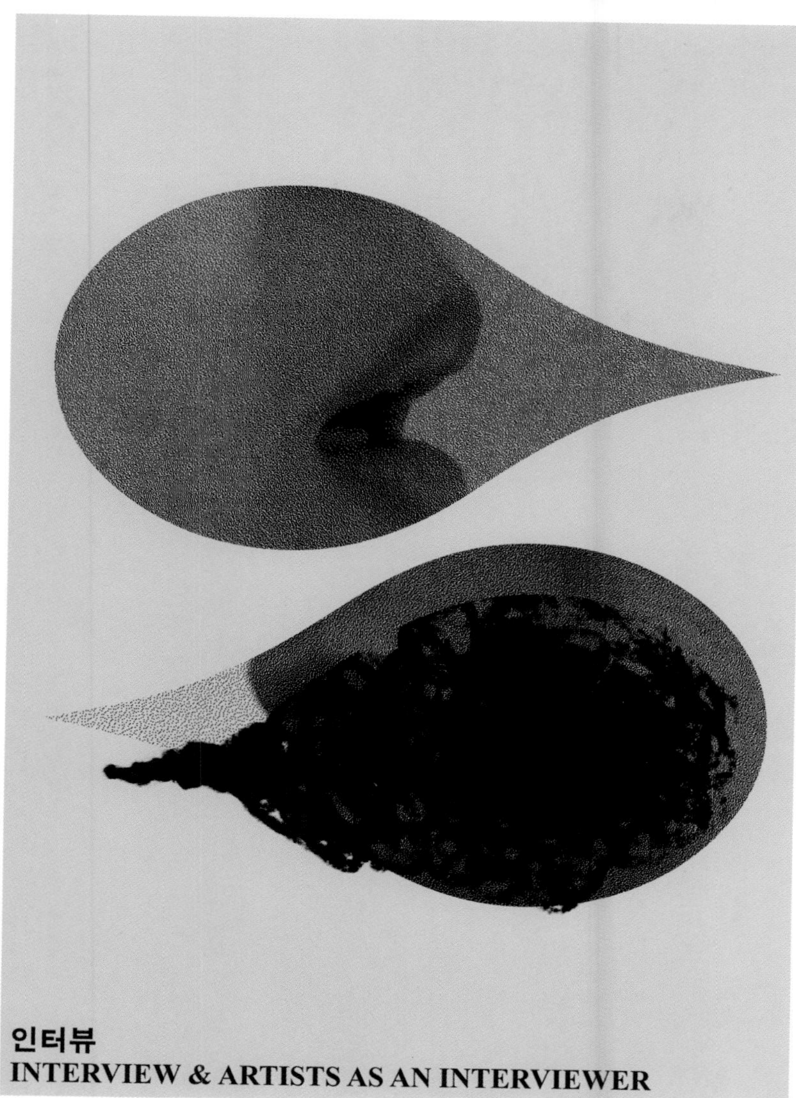

Typeface in Use
Times New Roman Bold

"This is the poster for the exhibition about an interview. We have tried to show the meaning of 'INTER-VIEW' in a matter-of-fact way on the poster. So, we thought the typeface 'Times New Roman' is most proper for that."

INTERVIEW & ARTISTS AS AN INTERVIEWER
2011 — Poster, Advertisement, Invitation
Client Arko Art Center
Design TypePage (Jin Dallae, Park Woohyuk)

Typeface in Use
Times New Roman

"The content is taken from newspapers from the 60s and 70s. Therefore I chose Times New Roman."

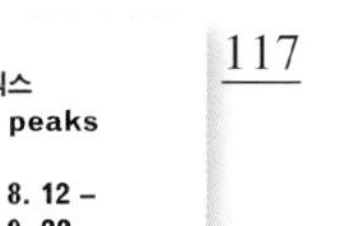

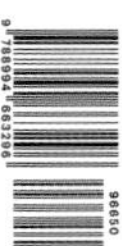

twin peaks
2012 — Book
Client Ryu, Biho (artist)
Design Shin, Dokho

The book is about the two vertices of the same newspaper. It shows it's both sides, the writer's work and the pure information transmitted by the newspaper.

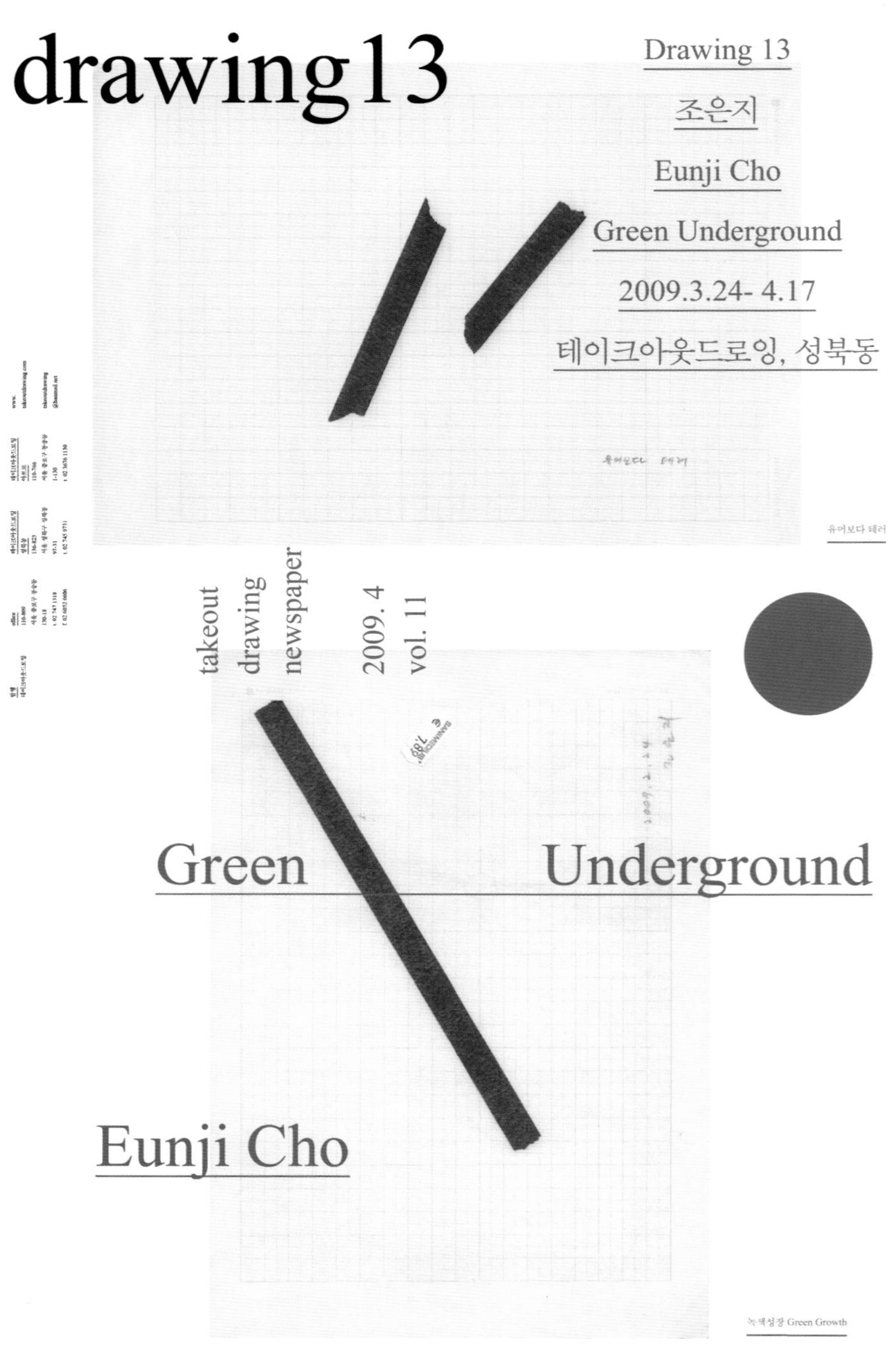
drawing13
Drawing 13
조은지
Eunji Cho
Green Underground
2009.3.24- 4.17
테이크아웃드로잉, 성북동
유머보다 테러
takeout
drawing
newspaper
2009. 4
vol. 11
Green Underground
Eunji Cho
녹색성장 Green Growth
design
Type Page
park woo-hyuk

Typeface in Use
Times New Roman Bold

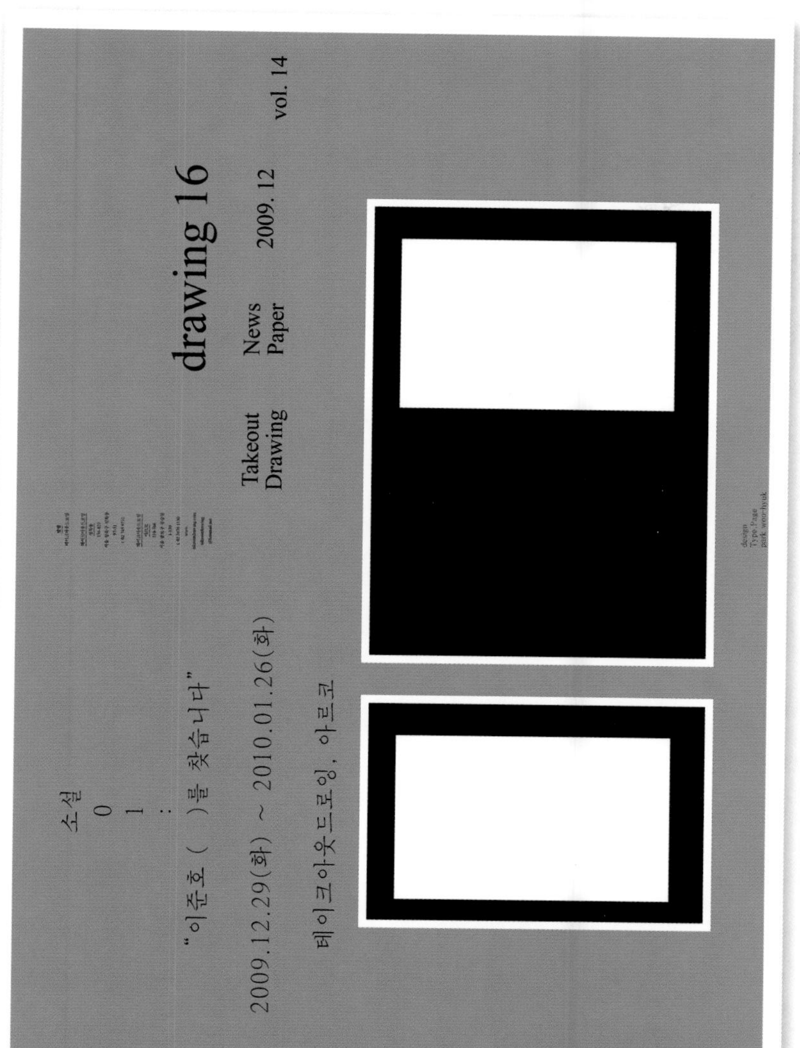

Takeout Drawing Newspaper
2009-12 — Newspaper, Poster
Client Cutural Space, Takeout Drawing
Design Type.Page (Jin Dallae, Park Woohyuk)

The 'Takeout Drawing' newspaper is published every two month and informs about various cultural events at Takeout Drawing.

TAKEOUT
DRAWING
NEWSPAPER

2012.6
Vol. 33

Takeout Drawing
683-139 Hannam-dong, Yongsan-gu
Seoul 140-892 Korea
t. 02 797 3139
www.takeoutdrawing.com
takeoutdrawing@hanmail.net

최은경 해열, 경景

DRAWING 35
CHOI EUNKYUNG
A REMEDY FOR
FEVER, LANDSCAPE
2012.6.22-7.19
TAKEOUT DRAWING
ITAEWON-DONG

DESIGN / TYPE.PAGE / www.typepage.com / 2012

Drawing 22
Takeout Drawing
Newspaper
2010. 9
vol. 20
옥인
콜렉티브
Okin
Collective
콘크리트
아일랜드
Concrete
Island
2010.09.01 –
2010.09.30
takeout drawing
hannam-dong

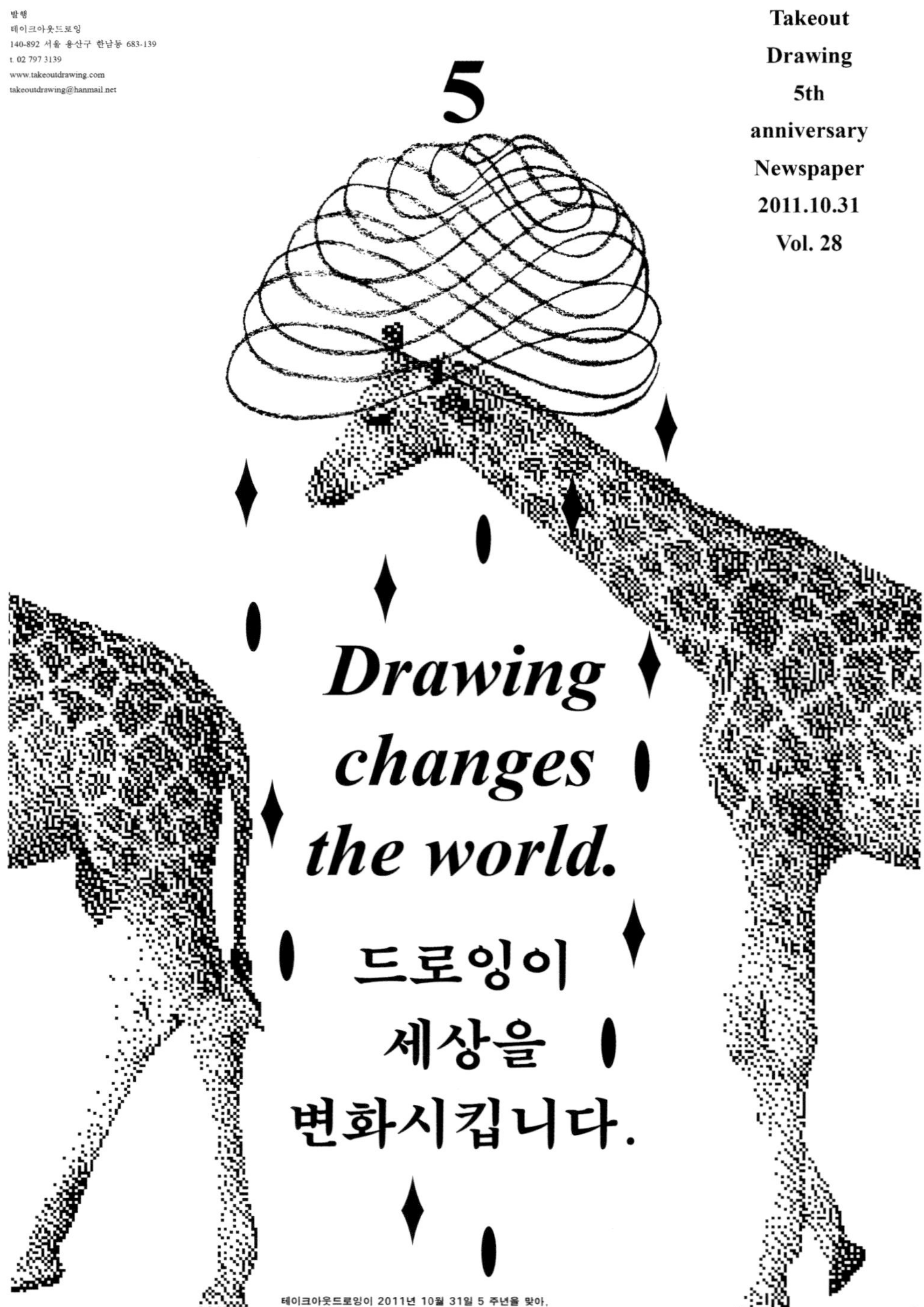

발행
테이크아웃드로잉
140-892 서울 용산구 한남동 683-139
t. 02 797 3139
www.takeoutdrawing.com
takeoutdrawing@hanmail.net

Takeout Drawing 5th anniversary Newspaper 2011.10.31 Vol. 28

5

Drawing changes the world.

드로잉이 세상을 변화시킵니다.

테이크아웃드로잉이 2011년 10월 31일 5 주년을 맞아,
드로잉에 관한 한 문장을 선물로 받아 이를 5주년 기념 특별판 신문에 소개합니다.

1

TAKEOUT DRAWING NEWSPAPER 2012.3 Vol. 29

Drawing that changes the world, Seoul 2012

세상을 바꾸는 드로잉 2012 서울

DRAWING THAT CHANGES THE WORLD 2012.3.23 - 2013.2.20

Takeout Drawing Hannam-dong & Itaewon-dong 세상을 바꾸는 드로잉

Typeface in Use
Times New Roman Bold

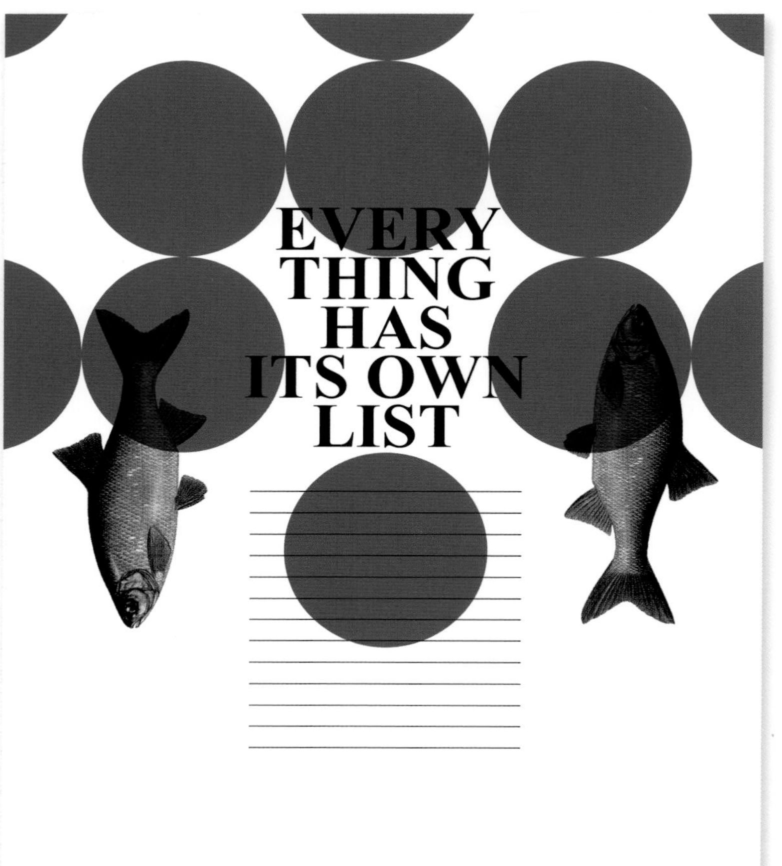

Everything has its own list
2012 — Book Design, Poster
Client Åland
Design workroom
Co-editor mediabus

This book we published together with the clothing multi-shop Åland. It has been produced with the participation of over 50 artists and designers and the multi-shop itself. There is a part like an obituary, a list of things in a time capsule, a list of real estates in the Hague, and a very nostalgic piece, such as a list of construction materials that are not produced anymore. We needed formal consistency to be able to deal with the inconsistent pieces of text. They needed to look like useful lists or completely useless gossip. Times New Roman, originally designed for a British newspaper, couldn't be better for such "disguise." A newspaper is originally a vessel to keep something great and rubbish together, and it is a huge editing machine in itself.

EVERY THING HAS ITS OWN LIST

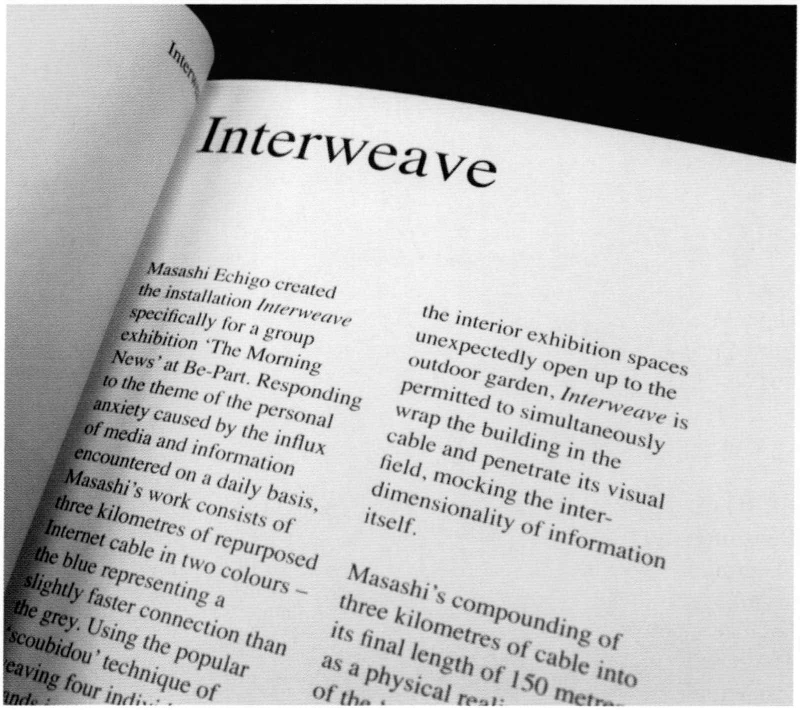

Masashi Echigo, Stories
2011 — Book Design
Client Masashi Echigo / Be-Part
Design Jurgen Maelfeyt

This book functions as a documentation instrument for the projects by Masashi Echigo whose work only exists temporary.

Typeface in Use
Times

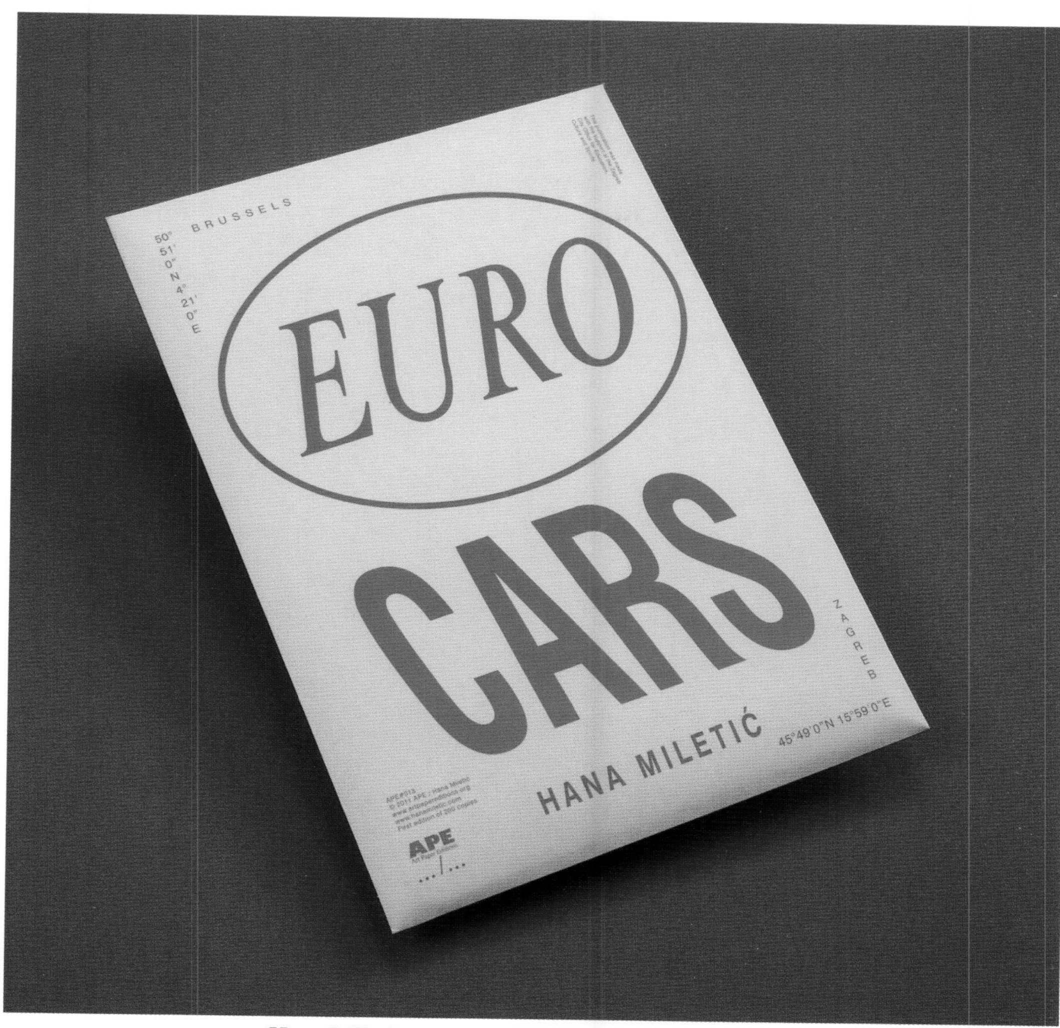

Hana Miletic,
Euro Cars
2011 — Book Design
Client Hana Miletic
Design Jurgen Maelfeyt

EURO Cars (Hana Miletic) is a collection of photographs of Mercedes-Benz brand cars with a no longer acceptable production date with regard to permitted European Union emission limits, better known as the "EURO norm" stages. With the directives and laws becoming stricter vehicles not meeting criteria can no longer be sold or imported into the Union. The series was photographed in Zagreb and in Brussels, both outside and inside the EU borders. The catalog is a collection of cards with technical codes on the backside.

George
Condo
353
Crown
Street
March
2
Room
C220
12:30pm

Typeface in Use
Times NRMT

S

George Condo
2010 — Poster
Client Yale
Design Keri Bronk

George Condo has a way of making you realize that people are really funny looking. To announce his visit to the painting department at Yale, artist Brendan Smith and I painted our faces and digitally manipulated the photograph — appropriating his work with tools that were familiar to us.

Keri Bronk's Favorite Times Letter is "S".

Portable – *A Process*

Portable — A Process
2012 — Maxi Cover
Client Live At Robert Johnson
Design Doeller & Satter

Massimiliano Pagliara —
Focus For Infinity
2012 — LP Cover
Client Live At Robert Johnson
Design Doeller & Satter

Massimiliano Pagliara
Focus For Infinity

Vinyl 1
A1 — *As The Night Breathes (feat. Heidi Diehl & Steve Gunn)*
A2 — *I'll Never Be*
B1 — *Harmonize*
B2 — *In Order Of More Depth*

Vinyl 2
C1 — *Gonna Get Your Love Gonna Find You (feat. Sigrid Elliott)*
C2 — *Fade The Light (feat. Mavin)*
D1 — *After*
D2 — *A Wrong Chance*

Right Page

If I Can't Dance, I Don't Want To Be Part Of Your Revolution
2010 — Poster
Client If I Can't Dance, I Don't Want To Be Part Of Your Revolution, Amsterdam
Design Maureen Mooren

Poster for the event "From dusk till dawn".

IF I CAN'T DANCE,
I DON'T WANT TO BE PART OF YOUR REVOLUTION

EDITION III
MASQUERADE

FROM
DUSK
TILL
DAWN

19 – 20 MARCH 2010
5 PM – 11 AM
VAN ABBEMUSEUM

LARS BANG LARSEN, RUTH BUCHANAN, YANN CHATEIGNÉ TYTELMAN, KEREN CYTTER, YAEL DAVIDS,
JON MIKEL EUBA, OLIVIER FOULON, LUCA FREI, AURÉLIEN FROMENT

SUCHAN KINOSHITA, JOACHIM KOESTER, MARIA PASK, PEGGY PHELAN, SARAH PIERCE,
JIMMY ROBERT, SUELY ROLNIK, STEFANIE SEIBOLD

WWW.IFICANTDANCE.ORG / WWW.VANABBEMUSEUM.NL
FROM DUSK TILL DAWN IS PART OF PLAY VANABBE

Benedikt Frey —
Running In Circles
2012 — Maxi Cover
Client Live At Robert Johnson
Design Doeller & Satter

8 80319 60151 4
Benedikt Frey – Running In Circles
A: Running In Circles, B: Closer
Written and produced by Benedikt Frey.
Vocals and rhodes on "Closer"
written and performed by A Forest.
Mastered by Lupo at D&M, Berlin.
Live At Robert Johnson, 2012.
Distribution: Kompakt. Graphic design:
Doeller & Satter.
Made in the EU. (playrjc022)
L
A R
J

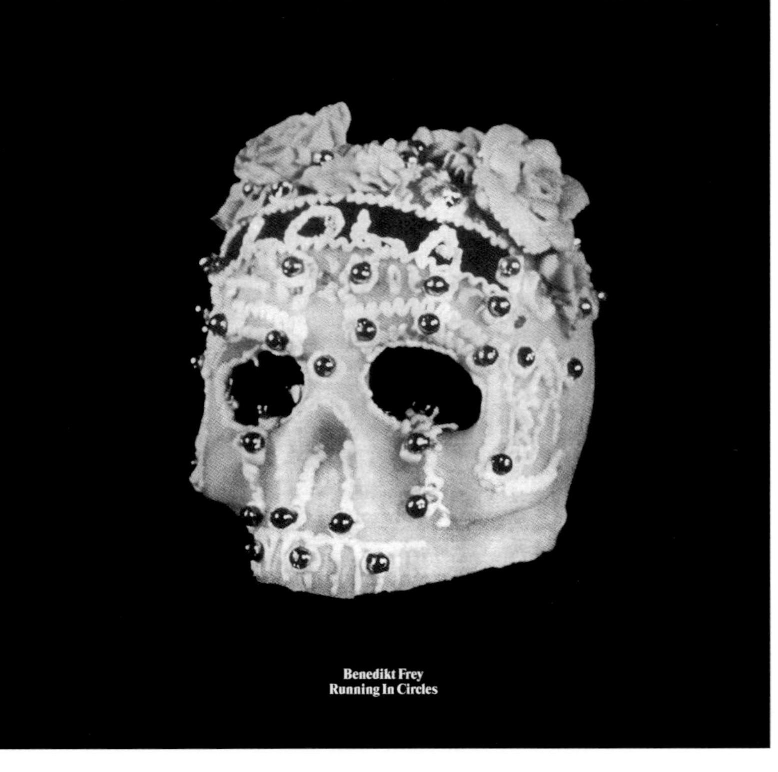

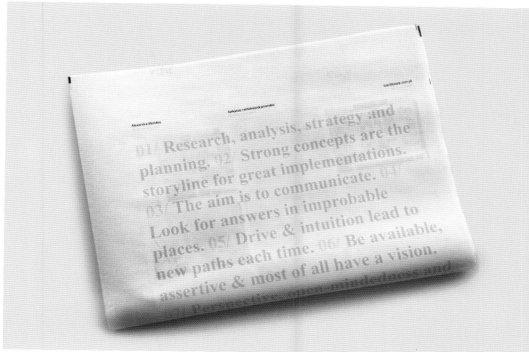

Blank Journal
2012 — Editorial Design
Design Blank (Alexandra Mendes)

Blank Journal is a promotional piece covering Blank's work, design thinking and approach to the creative process. Blank stands for Design Thinking For Graphic Minds, focusing on making tailored projects. By filling the blanks with fresh, provocative ideas, Blank intends to bring content to the table. The aim is to communicate!

"Blank's visual identity uses Akzidenz Grotesk as a bold, clear, sans-serif typeface which has no intrinsic meaning in its form, suitable for Blank design thinking. Le Blank Journal applies a similar principle when it combines Helvetica — a neutral, clean, sans-serif typeface — with Times New Roman — a classical serif typeface — two massively used fonts in the digital era. Blank Journal makes a statement on the front cover by simply displaying a blank block of typography over a block of color to communicate Blank's profile, a consultancy standing for Design Thinking For Graphic Minds."

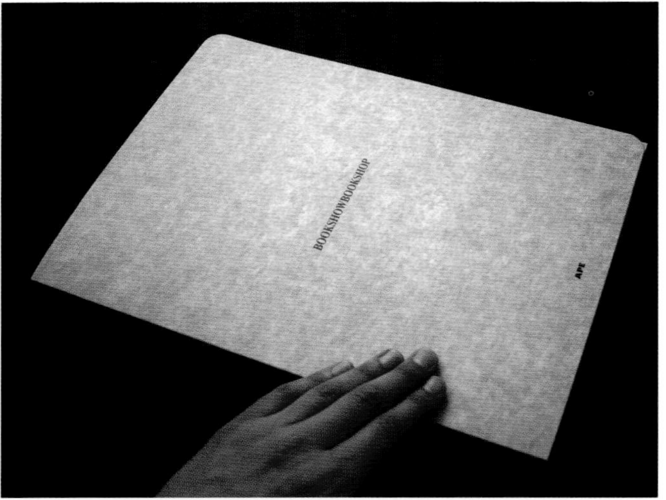

Jurgen Maelfeyt's Favorite Times Letter is "T".

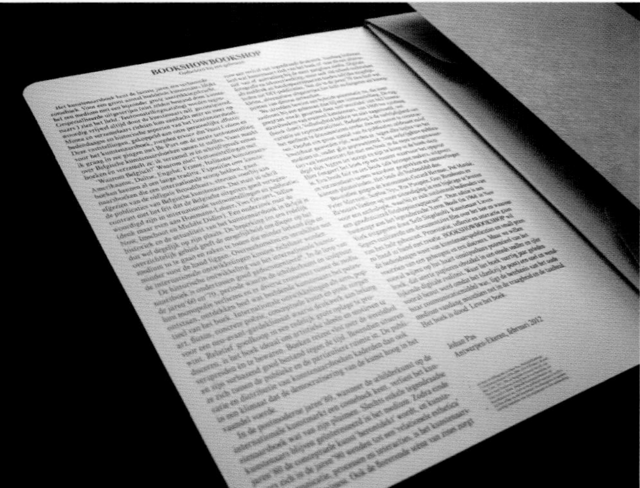

Typeface in Use
Times New Roman Bold Condensed

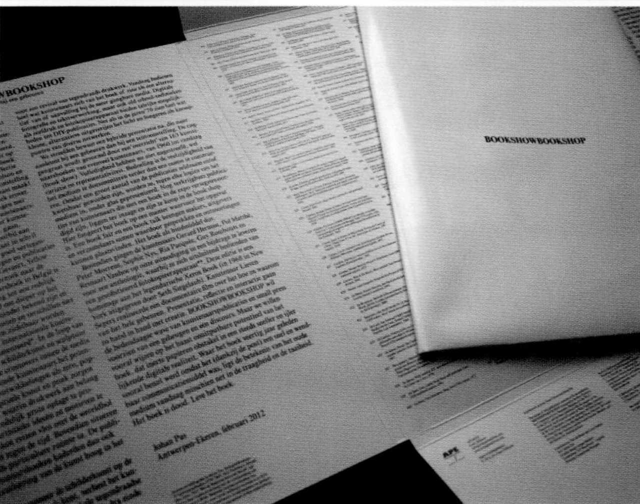

Book Show Book Shop
2012 — Book Design, Posters
Client Waregem / Be-Part
Design Jurgen Maelfeyt

This is a poster catalog showing all covers included in the exhibition about artist books.

Platform voor actuele kunst
BE PART
Westerlaan 17, B 8790 Waregem
+32 (0) 56 62 94 10
info@be-part.be
www.be-part.be

V.U. Patrick Delanoeye, Directeur, Grafisch Ontwerp: Jurgen Maelfeyt

15.04 — 10.06.2012

BOOK SHOW BOOK SHOP

Belgische kunstenaarsboeken van Verheyen tot vandaag

RICOH

POLISHING THE GOODS
DIAMONDS
BEAUTIFULLY GIFT BOXED FOR YOUR LOVED ONES
COCKTAIL RING
STAR OF GLORY SOLITAIRE DIAMOND
MARQUIS-SHAPED
MORNING LIGHT STAR SAPPHIRES
WISHING
QUALITY-CRAFTED IN THE FINEST OF PRECIOUS METALS AND STONES
SHOUT OUT FOR THE LADIES
TRUSTWORTHY

Times DB
2006 — Type Design
Design Hilary Greenbaum

Times DB was created as a display addition to the Times New Roman family.

Kimberly Meenan
Fighting The Urge To Pray
Medium: Installation

Vernissage Do, 08.10. 19 h
Finissage Sa, 31.10. 17 h

Kunstraum Winterthur
Raum für zeitgenössische Kunst
www.kunstraumwinterthur.ch

Kimberly
Meenan:
Fighting The
Urge To Pray
Kunstraum
Winterthur
08.10—31.10

Gloor & Jandl

Wildbachstrasse 7
8400 Winterthur
Mi, Sa 15–18 h / Do 18–21 h

ERNST GÖHNER STIFTUNG
Fondation Nestlé pour l'Art
KULTURSTIFTUNG WINTERTHUR
Stadt Winterthur

Typeface in Use
Times Ten

Poster Kunstraum Winterthur
2010 — Poster
Client Kunstraum Winterthur, Winterthur CH
Design Gloor & Jandl

This poster is part of a whole variety of printed matter for an offspace art gallery near Zurich. The printed exposure of the currently exhibiting artists appears as an all-purpose poster. This strict and multifunctional adaption arises from the low budget and allows to operate within short-termed commissions.

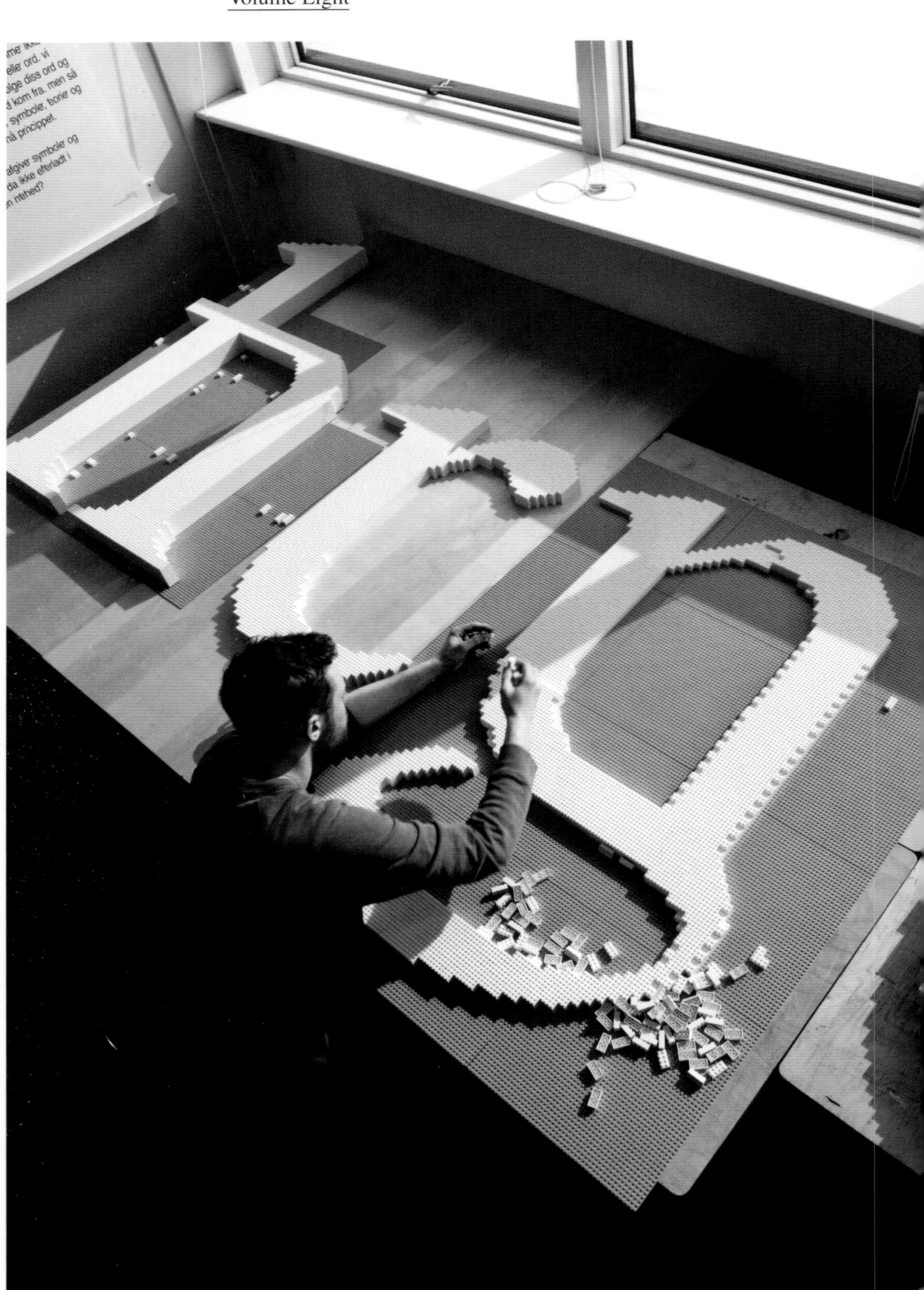
elle ord. vi
olge diss ord og
kom fra. men så
symboler, teorier og
nå princippet.
afgive symboler og
da ikke efterladt i
n nehed?

eve·yhŋ written symbols can say has alcady passd by. hey ac like tracks left by animals. hat is ʁy he masters of meditation cfus to accept hat writŋs ac fnal. he aim is to cach true bŋ by means of hos tracks, hos signs – but itslf is not a sign, and it leaves no tracks. it doesn't come to us by way of letters or words. we can go toward it, by followŋ hos words and letters back to ʁat hey came from. but so loŋ as we ac pcoccupied wih symbols, heories and opinions, we will fail to cach he prnciple.

— but ʁen we give up symbols and opinions, acn't we left n utter nohŋness of bŋ?

— yes

Kimura Kyūho
-On the myssteries of Swordsmanship
1768

Typeface in Use
Times New Roman

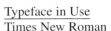

"When working with the basic elements of the alphabet, I needed to focus on the letterforms themselves and not the font. I chose to work with Helvetica and Times New Roman since these are the modern arch types of Antiqua and Grotesque typefaces. That way I was able to test the new letters in both style of types. For example the 'g' letter is very different in the two categories."

The Betabet
2012 — Conceptual Typography, Exhibition
Design Birk Marcus Hansen

My Bachelor project was a development of Betabet, a typeface that took a study of our phonetic and visual use of the Latin alphabet as its starting point. By combining two letters, I studied how far we can go in terms of decoding the latin alphabet.

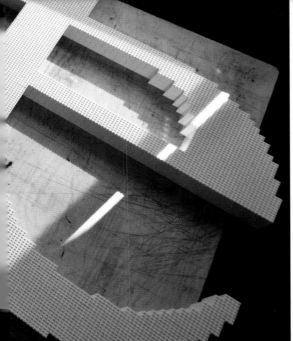

Rule
Book

Rule
Book
Rule
Book
No
reading

Closed
on
Mondays

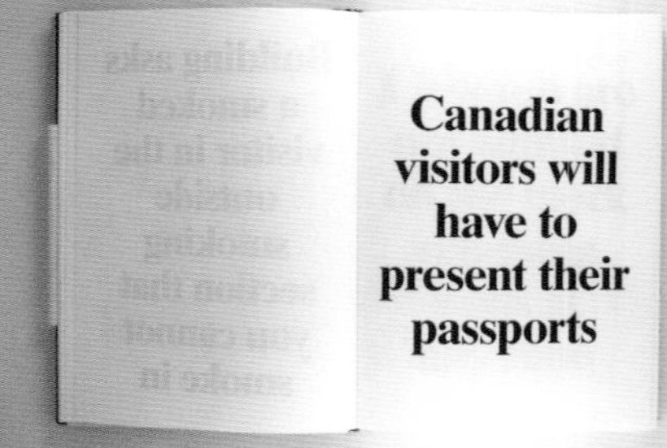
Canadian
visitors will
have to
present their
passports

Be
Brief

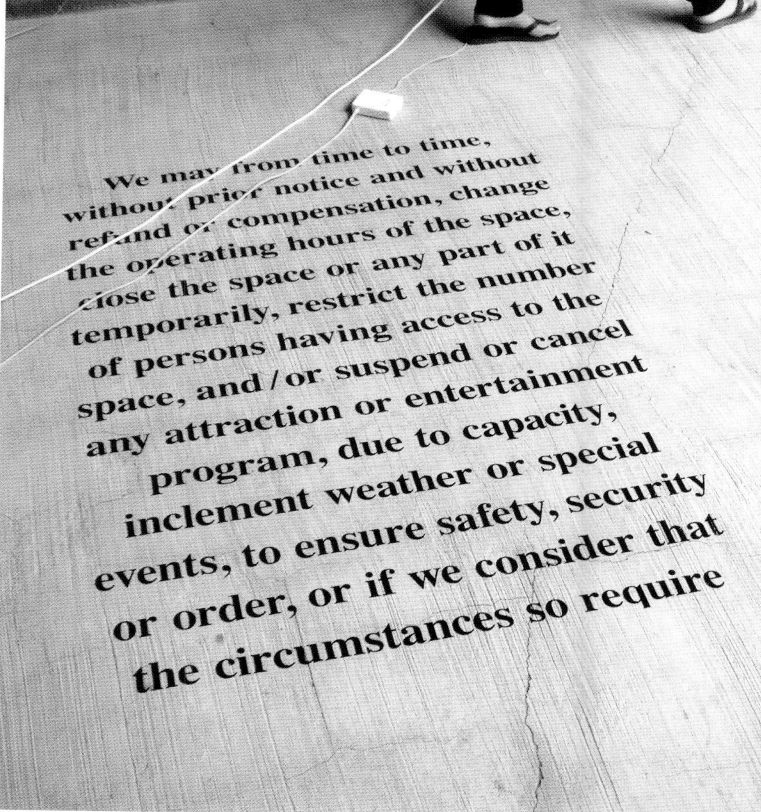

We may from time to time,
without prior notice and without
refund or compensation, change
the operating hours of the space,
close the space or any part of it
temporarily, restrict the number
of persons having access to the
space, and / or suspend or cancel
any attraction or entertainment
program, due to capacity,
inclement weather or special
events, to ensure safety, security
or order, or if we consider that
the circumstances so require

Rule Book
2010 — Book Design, Installation
Design Hyo Kwon
Collaboration Goda Budvytyte, Isabelle Vaverka, Gregory Dapra

This project started as a workshop "Transform the workshop building into a public space" given by James Goggin and Maureen Mooren. During the process, we revolved around a question "What makes a space a public space?" and we believed that what defines a public space are the activities that happen within the space that are dictated by rules which service the space's purpose and function.

As a result, an installation was made on the floor of the workshop space as an attempt to define the space by giving it a set of rules. Over 300 rules were collected from various sources and later compiled in a book in an alphabetical order.

e

Hyo Kwon's Favorite Times Letter is "e".

Typeface in Use
Times Ten

"Since this project was about rules found in public space, we wanted to use a typeface that is widely used and looks official. Having this in mind, it was a natural decision for us to choose Times in order to imitate the default aesthetic that can easily be found on the streets."

2

Moderna by N…

I betrak…
23 april…

Hans Caldaras…
Marin Alexand…
Rosa Taikon, Y…
Dorinel Marc, …
Gülsün Karam…
Dj Simina Astil…

ROSA TAIKON, SILVERKONST-

Å ANDRA SIDAN

MODERNA BY NIGHT

SAMTIDA ROMSK KULTUR

3

Moderna by N…

Välkom…
till Kjar…
7 maj 18…

Kjartan Sletten…
Kate Pendry, C…
Luke Fowler, G…
Premiär! Kjart…
DV, 2004, av P…
Wannefors. Dj…

MODERNA BY NIGHT

VÄLKOMMEN TILL KJARTANISTAN!

MODERNA BY NIGHT

5

Moderna by Night

International Short Film Festival Oberhausen 50 years 26 November 18-01

Artists' films & videos from the festival archive. Jayne Parker, London. Martín Mejía, Göteborg. Anna Linder, Cecilia Lundqvist, Michel Wenzer, Sten Sandell, David Stackenäs, Stockholm. Filmer av Martin Arnold, Robert Cahen, Marina Grzinic, Takashi Ito, Matthias Müller, Anna Thew, Jan Verbeek.

Entré 80 kr, studenter och MMV 60 kr. Antal biljetter till försäljning är 350. Förköp i Butiken på Moderna Museet. Curator: Catrin Lundqvist i samarbete med Reinhard W. Wolf, International Short Film Festival Oberhausen, Filmform och Goethe-Institutet. Grafisk design och scenografi: Research and Development.

MODERNA BY NIGHT

FILM, VIDEO OCH MUSIK

FESTIVALEN I OBERHAUSEN 50 ÅR

FILMFORM STOCKHOLM

SAMTIDA FILM OCH VIDEO

PROGRAM

MODERNA BY NIGHT

FILM, VIDEO AND MUSIC

50 YEARS OF THE OBERHAUSEN FESTIVAL

FILMFORM STOCKHOLM

CONTEMPORARY FILM AND VIDEO

PROGRAM

MODERNA MUSEET

Typeface in Use
Moderna Museet Times

"The Times used is a part of the corporate identity of the Moderna Museet, Stockholm."

Moderna by Night
2004 — Program, Newspaper, Poster, Set Design
Client Moderna Museet, Stockholm
Design Research and Development (Daniel Olsson, Jonas Topooco)

Identity and set design for Moderna by Night at Moderna Museet, Stockholm. A series of happenings taking place during closing hours. The museums existing lighting was switched off and replaced by construction floodlights.

Moderna
by Night
Hommage à
Meret Oppenheim

Moderna
by Night
26 mars, 23 april, 7 maj,
10 sept, 26 nov
Design: Research and

OPPRESSIO
29 MEI – 24 JUNI 2007
HOLLAND FESTI
HF

Holland Festival
2007 — Poster
Client Holland Festival
Design Maureen Mooren

Poster campaign for the yearly event Holland Festival.

Typeface in Use
Times New Roman,
Helvetica Neue TT Bold,
DTL Elzevir T Caps Regular,
Nobel Regular,
Stop Regular

HOLLAND FESTIVAL
COM
29 MEI – 24 JUNI 2007

T

Research and Development's Favorite Times Letter is "T".

"An everyday type for everyday stories."

Typeface in Use
Times

An Alternative Guide to Palais de Tokyo
2006 — Guidebook
Client Palais de Tokyo, Paris
Design Research and Development
(Daniel Olsson, Jonas Topooco)

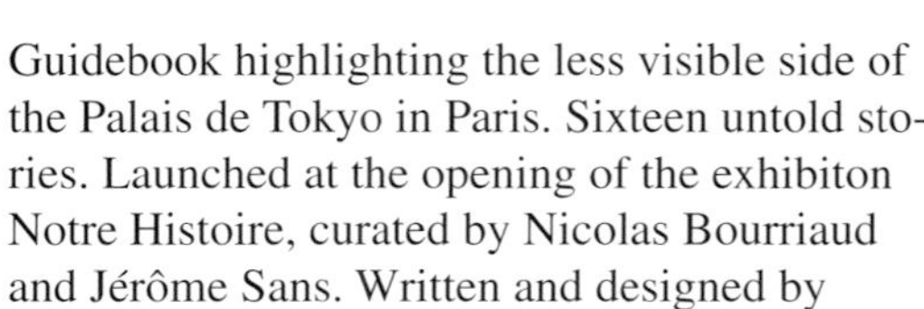

Guidebook highlighting the less visible side of the Palais de Tokyo in Paris. Sixteen untold stories. Launched at the opening of the exhibiton Notre Histoire, curated by Nicolas Bourriaud and Jérôme Sans. Written and designed by Research and Development.

An Alternative Guide to Palais de Tokyo

by Research and Development

The Secret Life of an Art Institution

Do Not Keep This Book 11/5/2018 - 11/7/2018
THIS BOOK IS FREE
BY
ACCEPTING
THIS BOOK
YO EE
T D
CON IONS
OF THIS
BOOK.
352/500

Typeface in Use
Times NRMT

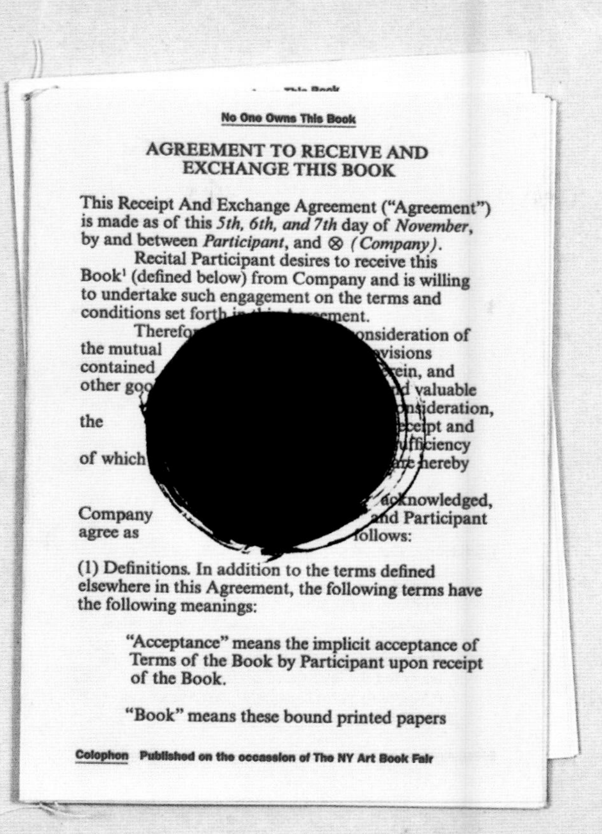

No One Owns This Book

AGREEMENT TO RECEIVE AND EXCHANGE THIS BOOK

This Receipt And Exchange Agreement ("Agreement") is made as of this *5th, 6th, and 7th* day of *November*, by and between *Participant*, and ⊗ *(Company)*.

Recital Participant desires to receive this Book[1] (defined below) from Company and is willing to undertake such engagement on the terms and conditions set forth … ment.

Therefo… nsideration of the mutual … visions contained … ein, and other go… d valuable … nsideration, the … ceipt and … fficiency of which … re hereby … knowledged, Company … nd Participant agree as … follows:

(1) Definitions. In addition to the terms defined elsewhere in this Agreement, the following terms have the following meanings:

"Acceptance" means the implicit acceptance of Terms of the Book by Participant upon receipt of the Book.

"Book" means these bound printed papers

Colophon Published on the occassion of The NY Art Book Fair

Agreement to Receive and Exchange
2010 — Book Design
Design Keri Bronk, Ryan Weafer

At the 2010 New York Art Book Fair, several exhibitors proposed using books as a type of currency. As a form of intervention, this book served as a loop-hole currency — a book solely meant for trading. We distributed our book for free explaining it was a type of voucher that could be traded for another book inside with the hopes of flooding the market and filling the aforementioned vendors' libraries with our book. The book took the form of a contract, which upon receipt bound the recipient to a number of terms including non-ownership, responsibility to exchange, and agreement that our project met the minimum requirement for a book.

Enquêtes (1, 2, 3, 4, 5, 6, 7, 8, 9)

De Proeftuin
2009 — Publication
Client Inge Stolwijk
Design Kees Bakker

"How would you describe the average Dutch person?" De Proeftuin, by Inge Stolwijk, is a photographic investigation with this question in mind. The publication contains portraits of the (supposedly) average Dutch person, environmental shots of the (supposedly) average Dutch town, Woerden, and has an interview section with its citizens, together making you wonder if there is even such a thing as average.

Typeface in Use
Times New Roman,
Akzidenz Grotesk BE

"Times New Roman seemed to fit the subject of the book, 'being average', perfectly."

"Boven het gemiddelde uit willen steken is een goed streven, denk ik."

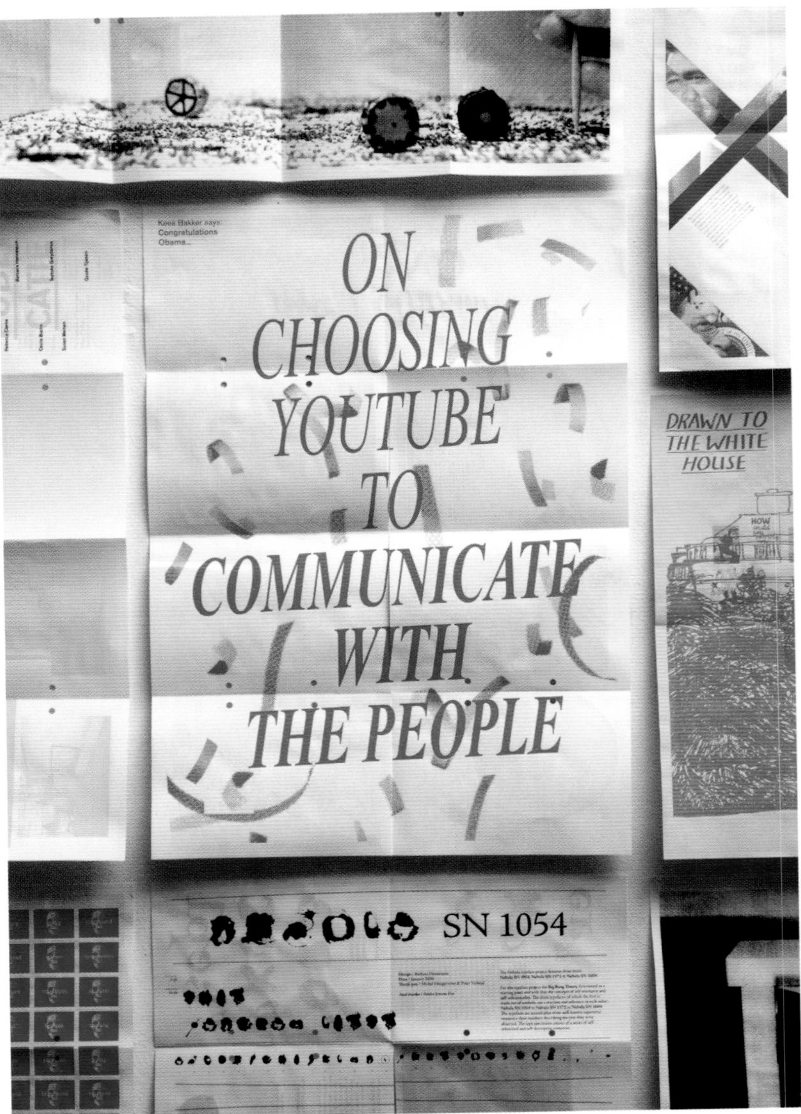

Collective Publication
2009 — Posters, Publication
Design Kees Bakker, Rebecca Clarke, Siebe Bluijs, Gauke Tijssen, Barbara Hennequin, Teatske Greijdanus, Susan Meinen, Cecile Bosch.

The Collective Publication is a publication/poster which has been silkscreened in collaboration with seven Royal Academy of Art students. The pieces were handfolded, manually hole punched and bound together with binder clips. The theme of the publication was 'current events in the news', which in Kees Bakker's case was the inauguration of Barack Obama. The publication consists of eight eclectic and colorful A2 posters, which folded and bound together create an equally eclectic and colorful publication.

Typeface in Use
Times New Roman,
Akzidenz Grotesk BE

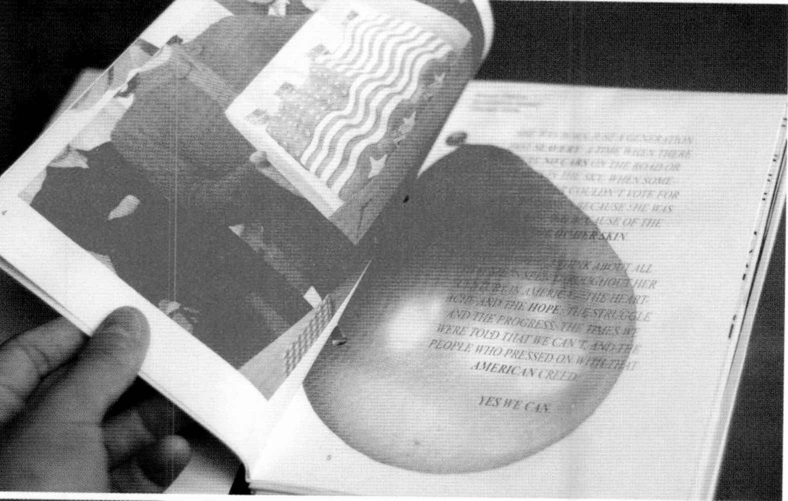

"These two typefaces, in capitals, condensed, stretched and outlined are a great representation of America."

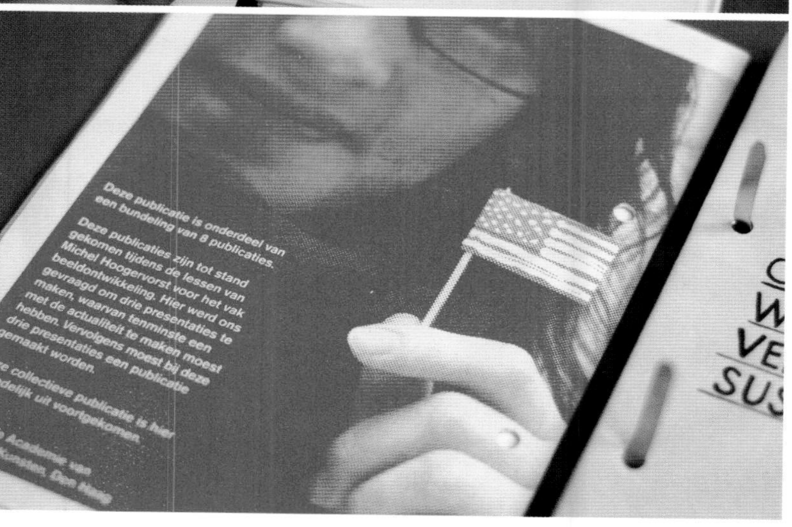

Ahonen & Lamberg
ahonenandlamberg.com

Ahonen & Lamberg is a multidisciplinary design studio based in Paris. Founded in 2006 by Finnish designers Anna Ahonen and Katariina Lamberg, it concentrates on art direction, creative consultancy and graphic design covering a wide range of areas and an equally vast client list ranging from multinational companies, magazines or luxury brands to emerging artists and fashion designers. The Ahonen & Lamberg design principle is to balance classical and alternative design, creating a tone that is always elegant, recognisable and yet eager to surprise.
— p. 48-49

Anna Haas
annahaas.ch

Anna Haas works as a graphic designer, art director and illustrator with a focus on book design. She has worked in Belgium, Germany and the Netherlands, but lives since 2011 in Zürich, Switzerland.
— pp. 16-19

Blank
blank.com.pt

Blank focuses on making tailored projects. Approaching each one individually, with a concept oriented, analytical thinking mind. Experimentation is the basic structure of the work. Looking to find engaging design solutions to implement meaningful communication strategies. From concept through completion.
— p. 133

Birch
birchstudio.co.uk

Birch is a London based design studio working in diverse areas of communication design including art direction, book design, identity and branding, moving image and web based projects. Their process begins with a research led approach through a close relationship with the client to inform the details of the distinctive typographic and visual work.
— p. 81

Birk Marcus Hansen
birkmarcus.dk

Birk Marcus Hansen is a graphic design student at the Kolding School of Design, Denmark. He has been working a semester in New York, done a cooperation ith LEGO, was comissioned to create visuals for the Expo 2010 in Shanghai, touring with bands in China, Germany and Denmark, and created video art for the opera “Tomorrow in a Year” by Hotel Pro Forma.
— pp. 138-139

Burri-Preis
burri-preis.ch

Burri-Preis are two graphic designers based in Zurich, Switzerland. They are collaborating since 2008 on printed matter, such as books, posters, logos, flyers and sometimes they even do websites.
— pp. 92-93, 104-109

Catalogue
thisiscatalogue.co.uk

Catalogue is an independent graphic design studio founded in 2010 in the North of England. We specialise in design for print, branding, identity, books, exhibition and web. We work for both commercial clients and on self initiated projects.
— p. 28

Catrin Sonnabend
catrinsonnabend.de

Catrin Sonnabend is a graphic designer based in Berlin. Her projects vary from commissioned pieces such as books, magazines, posters, illustrations, corporate design and animations to collaborations with different design studios as well as self initiated work. After studying at Hochschule für Gestaltung, Offenbach (Germany) she worked for several studios such as Stiletto, Scrollan, Bureau Mario Lombardo and Pixelgarten before she founded her own studio in 2009.
— pp. 50-51

Chris Steurer
csteurer.com

Chris Steurer has been working as a designer since 1997, he has initiated and directed projects focussing on contemporary visual identity and its implementation in various media. In order to communicate as effectively and efficiently as possible, he endeavors to define an expressive language providing both relevance and resonance.
— pp. 34-35

Cox & Grusenmeyer
cox-grusenmeyer.com

Cox & Grusenmeyer is an Antwerp based design studio, founded by Ines Cox and Lauren Grusenmeyer. They started collaborating at the Sint-Lucas Ghent design school and continued working together while Cox completed her master at the Werkplaats Typografie in Arnhem and Grusenmeyer at the Sandberg Institute in Amsterdam. Being a duo, operating together and against each other, they use their collaboration as a tool for dialog and confrontation and as a platform to share ideas.
— pp. 98-99, 160-161

Doeller & Satter
doeller-satter.com

Doeller & Satter is a graphic design studio based in Frankfurt am Main. The studio mainly works on books, art catalogues, magazines, and posters. It also develops logotypes, corporate design, branding, and websites. Doeller & Satter works both for clients and on self-initiated projects.
— pp. 40-41, 129-130, 132

Elio Salichs
salichs.net

Elio Salichs is an independent graphic designer based in Barcelona. He founded his one-member studio in 2011. Since then he has been working across a variety of media and fields, from brand identity to websites. He believes in conceptual and simple design solutions.
— pp. 30-31

Fasett
fasett.no

Fasett is a communications agency which creates value for its clients through courage, knowledge and commitment. They are independent and give their clients advice without being tied to a particular technological solution.
— pp. 32-33

Felix Pfäffli
feixen.ch

Feixen is the graphic design work of Felix Pfäffli. Felix was born in 1986. In 2010 he graduated and started his own studio "Feixen". In the summer of 2011 he was appointed as teacher at the Lucerne School of Graphic Design to teach in the fields of typography, narrative design, and poster design.
— pp. 56- 59

Gloor & Jandl
hannesgloor.biz

Hannes Gloor graduated from the Zurich University of the Arts in 2007. Since then he has been working as a graphic designer for a broad range of clients, mostly in collaboration with Stefan Jandl. His work consists of printed matter such as books, magazines and posters.
— pp. 52-53, 137

Hilary Greenbaum
hilarygreenbaum.com

Hilary Greenbaum is a New York-based graphic designer, writer and professor. She is currently the design director for the Whitney Museum of American Art. Her work has been recognized by the Society of Publication Designers, the Type Directors Club, AIGA, the Society for News Design and the Output Foundation. She also holds a MFA in design from the California Institute of the Arts.
— p. 136

Homework
homework.dk

Homework is a creative agency and design consultancy offering visual brand identity, packaging and advertising for the art, culture, fashion and luxury industry. Homework was founded in 2005 by Jack Dahl. He has worked as art director for mens fashion magazine HE, Intermission and Cover magazine. In addition, Jack Dahl has worked with Self Service magazine and the strategic and creative Paris agency Petronio Associates on a selection of fashion, beauty and luxury brands.
— pp. 72-75

Hyo Kwon
hyokwon.org

Hyo Kwon is a graphic designer currently based in NY. She graduated from the Royal Academy of Art (KABK) in The Hague in 2007 and has worked as a designer at Studio KABK until entering Werkplaats Typografie in 2008. She lives now in NY and works on a wide range of both commissioned and self-initiated projects.
— pp. 140-141

Jurgen Maelfeyt
jurgenmaelfeyt.be

Jurgen Maelfeyt studied graphic design at Sint-Lucas in Ghent (Belgium). In 2005 he started his own studio and works for cultural organizations, artists and publishers. In 2010 he founded APE (Art Paper Editions), a small independent publishing studio specializing in art, photography, illustration and typography.
— pp. 90-91, 110-111, 126-127, 134-135

Kees Bakker
likethesuitcase.com

After receiving his BA in graphic design at the Royal Academy of Art (KABK), Kees Bakker and his wife Rebecca Clarke (a gifted illustrator) moved to New York in late 2009. Kees now works as an independent designer based in Long Island City, New York. Besides continuing to work with clients in the cultural and fashion field, Kees has the mission to become a motivating and talented professor for future design students in the United States.
— pp. 38-39, 152-155

Keri Bronk
keribronk.com

Keri Bronk is a graphic designer based in New York City. She holds an MFA from Yale University and a degree in product design from Philadelphia University. She has taught at The University of the Arts in Philadelphia and been a visiting critic at St. Johns University, Parsons, International Center of Photography and Yale University.
— pp. 128, 150-151

Lesley Moore
lesley-moore.nl

Lesley Moore is the brainchild of Karin van den Brandt (1975, Blerick, The Netherlands) and Alex Clay (1974, Lørenskog, Norway). Since studying at the Arnhem Academy of the Arts (now ArtEZ) their careers have been intertwined. Early cooperations include the design for the Academy's magazine 'De Kunsten'. In 2004 they went on to form Lesley Moore, the name referring to 'less is more'. This mentality can be detected on various levels in their work, but first and foremost in the minimalistic approach in the conceptual phase of the creative process.
— pp. 88-89

Letra
letra.com.pt

Marco Balesteros is a graphic designer, editor and the founder of the design studio Letra. He has a Master Degree in Design and Typography by the Werkplaats Typografie, ArtEZ Institute of Arts, Arnhem. Simultaneously to the commissioned work, Marco develops editorial and educational projects concerning self-publishing together with Sofia Gonçalves.
— pp. 36-37

Maureen Mooren
maureenmooren.nl

Maureen Mooren is a graphic designer based in Amsterdam, the Netherlands, where she runs her own studio. In her work Mooren, by definition raises the issue of representation. In recent years Mooren has worked as an guest tutor at Werkplaats Typografie in Arnhem, the Netherlands.
— p. 131, 146-147

Monsieur Julien Martin
monsieurjulienmartin.tumblr.com

Julien Martin was born in 1984 in Saint-Tropez, France. He left home when he was 16, travelled for 4 years the country with an italian circus and finally reached Paris in 2004. He entered the École Nationale Supérieure des Beaux-Arts de Paris, but dropped out two years later to travel the south of Europe, Portugal, Spain and Italy. He lives currently in Paris.
— pp. 100-101

Mind Design
minddesign.co.uk

Established in 1999, Mind Design is a design consultancy that specialises in the development of visual identities which includes print, web, and interior design. The studio is run by Holger Jacobs and Stewart Walker. Their approach combines hands-on craftmanship, conceptual thinking and intuition and develop visual ideas on the basis of research into production processes or the use of unusual materials. Depending on the demands of a project they take advantage of their network of creative professionals.
— pp. 64-67

Mylinh Trieu Nguyen
mylinhtrieu.com

Mylinh Trieu Nguyen is a designer based in Miami Beach, FL. Her work explores ideas of distribution, collaboration and curation through new and appropriated systems and frameworks. She has a MFA in Graphic Design from Yale University, School of Art and a BFA in Design | Media Arts from the University of California, Los Angeles (UCLA). She is currently the Art Director at The Wolfsonian-FIU, a museum of design and material culture situated in the heart of South Beach.
— pp. 20-24, 102

Omar Nicolas, Maret Tholen, Haren Verleger
omarnicolas.de
hagenverleger. com

Omar Nicolas, Maret Tholen and Haren Verleger are students at the Muthesius Academy of Fine Arts and Design. They studied typography and graphic design in Kiel, Leipzig, Maastricht and Damascus.
— pp. 84-87

Post Projects
post-projects.com

Post Projects is a Vancouver based graphic art and design studio that began with the partnership of Alex Nelson and Beau House. They currently work with a network of local and international specialists on identity & branding, print media, and interactive development.The studio's philosophy "It could be better" is an oft-repeated phrase in the Post Projects studio. They understand the commercial value of good creative ideas and see great potential for development in today's visual landscape. They operate with a flexible, open process and appreciate working with people that are focused on craftsmanship.
— pp. 82-83

Raffinerie AG für Gestaltung
raffinerie.com

Raffinerie AG für Gestaltung was founded in March 2000. It is being directed by Reto Ehrbar and Nenad Kovacic (both founders and partners) and Christian Haas. They started small with three people, and grew constantly every year. At the moment they are 14 people, all graphic designers or illustrators. There is no such style as 'the Raffinerie style'. They try to come up with a new solution for every new client.
— pp. 46-47, 68-71, 70-73

Research and Development
researchanddevelopment.se

Art Director duo Daniel Olsson and Jonas Topooco in partnership since 2002. They work in close collaboration with artists, architects, curators, critics, collectors, directors, museums and cultural institutions.
— pp. 142-145, 148-149

Rob van den Nieuwenhuizen
drawswords.com

Amsterdam-based design studio Drawswords was founded in 2008 by graphic designer Rob van den Nieuwenhuizen. Drawswords designs for both cultural and commercial fields and works on visual identities, publications, editorial design, websites, music packaging, artist books, flyers and posters. The studio also initiates projects of its own, like the Langscapes collaborations with several well-known composers.
— pp. 42-45, 54-55

shin, dokho
shindokho.kr

Shin is a freelance designer. He enjoys collaborating with people of various fields, especially on typographic projects. He is based in Seoul.
— pp. 116-117

Stout / Kramer
stoutkramer.nl

Stout / Kramer has a special interest in the role the designer can take in the creative process. "We don't want to set ourselves up as merely designers of a message. We see ourselves as editors and directors of communication. As editor the designer interprets the content and context of a message. As director the designer is responsible for the appropriate means of communication. The final solutions are the result of an analytical and rational way of thinking and working. The design is simple, clear, without fuss. Dutch."
— pp. 112-113

Tankboys
tankboys.biz

Tankboys is a Venice-based independent design studio founded in 2005 by Lorenzo Mason and Marco Campardo. Tankboys' core activities consist of art direction, research, print, identity and editorial projects. Alongside with that, they give lectures, hold workshops and run a publishing house called Automatic Books.
— p. 29

thisislove studio
thisislove.pt

thisislove is a Lisbon based multidisciplinary design studio focused on communication design and experimental media projects.
— p. 80

Tsto
tsto.org

Tsto is a creative agency founded by six designers: Johannes Ekholm, Jonatan Eriksson, Inka Järvinen, Matti Kunttu, Jaakko Pietiläinen and Antti Uotila.
— pp. 76-77

twelve
threebyfour.org

12 is a London-based multidisciplinary design studio. Founded by a graphic designer, Shi Yuan and and economist, Rex Lifan Chen in 2009, 12 operates in and between fields of design, art, spatial practice and social affairs. Their design methodology has strong foundations in research and analysis, with an emphasis on typography.
— pp. 25-27

TwoPoints.Net
— Barcelona, Berlin
twopoints.net

TwoPoints.Net is specialized in flexible visual systems for Visual Identities. They are based in Barcelona and Berlin, but work mostly internationally.
— pp. 60-63. 94-97

Type.Page
typepage.com

The graphic design studio of Jin Dallae and Park Woo hyuk, Type Page, is located in Seoul. Their design is focused on social and cultural events and they keep on trying to find their own taste. They are publishing the typographic newspaper 'Archiv Peace' at their project space 'Archiv Peace'.
— pp. 103, 114-115, 118-123

Veronica Ditting
veronicaditting.com

Veronica Ditting (1979) is an independent graphic designer. She was born in Buenos Aires, Argentina, grew up in Germany and is currently working in Amsterdam and London. Veronica graduated from the Gerrit Rietveld Academy, Amsterdam in 2005 and since then worked for a diverse range of clients from individuals to institutions in the cultural field, focusing mainly on printed matter. She is the art director of the magazines The Gentlewoman and Fantastic Man. Her work has been awarded with the Best Dutch Book Designs and D&AD (British Design & Art Direction), and nominated for the Dutch Design Awards, Aica Awards a. o. Next to running her own studio, she taught at the Gerrit Rietveld Academy and Willem de Kooning Academy.
— pp. 10-15

workroom
workroom.kr

Located in Seoul, Korea, workroom is a graphic design studio and publishing house. In December 2006, four people—a photographer, an editor and two graphic designers—jointly opened the studio. Since then, workroom has primarily worked on community design and publishing as well as design services for clients. In addition, workroom helps run Gagarin, a second-hand bookstore opened in 2008 that specializes in art and design.
— pp. 78-79, 124-125

First published and distributed by
viction:workshop ltd.

viction:ary™

Unit C, 7th Floor, Seabright Plaza,
9-23 Shell Street, North Point, Hong Kong
URL: www.victionary.com
Email: we@victionary.com
www.facebook.com/victionworkshop
www.twitter.com/victionary_
www.weibo.com/victionary

Designed & Edited by TwoPoints.Net
Preface by Allan Haley & Jan Middendorp

Typefaces in Use:
Times LT Std Roman, Times LT Std Roman Italic

ISBN 978-988-19439-7-2

Printed and bound in China

We would like to thank all the designers and companies who made significant contribution to the compilation of this book. Without them this project would not be able to accomplish. We would also like to thank all the producers for their invaluable assistance throughout this entire proposal. The successful completion also owes a great deal to many professionals in the creative industry who have given us precious insights and comments. We are also very grateful to many other people whose names did not appear on the credits but have made specific input and continuous support the whole time.